THE PICTORIAL ATLAS OF
NORTH AMERICA'S
NATIONAL PARKS

THE PICTORIAL ATLAS OF
NORTH AMERICA'S
NATIONAL PARKS

Edited by
Marie Cahill and WJ Yenne

Brompton

First published in 1993 by
Brompton Books Corp.
15 Sherwood Place
Greenwich, CT 06830
USA

ISBN 0-86124-676-4

Printed in Hong Kong

Designed by Tom Debolski
Edited by Marie Cahill and WJ Yenne
Captioned by Marie Cahill .

Page 1: Crafted by nature's skilled hand, Delicate Arch in Arches National Park overwhelms with the impossibility of its creation.

Page 2-3: Mount Moran in Grand Teton National Park, Wyoming, rises majestically above Oxbow Bend on the Snake River.

Page 4-5: Grand Prismatic Spring at Yellowstone—the world's first national park.

TABLE OF CONTENTS

THE HISTORY OF THE NATIONAL PARKS IN NORTH AMERICA

By Marie Cahill

Since medieval times, parks—in one form or another—have been an essential part of man's existence. As early as 1079, William the Conqueror set aside The New Forest in southwestern Hampshire, England. In those days, parks functioned as private hunting reserves and consequently were preserved in their natural state so that wildlife could flourish, albeit to be hunted. Land outside the reserves was cultivated extensively and, sadly, many forms of plant and animal life risked extinction. Today, however, parks exist for *all* to enjoy, and in North America (as in most of the world) national parks have been established to protect large areas of lands encompassing some type of natural treasure—mountains, deserts, forests—as well as the wildlife that inhabits those areas.

In the United States, the 'national park idea' had its roots in the Washburn-Langford-Doane Expedition of 1870. Reports by hunters and trappers of strange and beautiful wonders in the Yellowstone region of the western United States inspired General Henry Washburn to lead an expedition to check out these tales of hot springs, petrified forests, spurting geysers, waterfalls, lakes and canyons. The members of the expedition found, much to their delight, that the reports were true, and naturally their thoughts turned to what should be done with this wondrous land. Their discussion centered on how the region should be divided so that it would reap the highest profit. However, Cornelius Hedges, a member of the party and later a Montana judge, was so impressed with the scenic beauty of the land that he proposed that it be set aside as a public park for all to enjoy.

Other people of the day shared Hedge's goal of protecting the nation's scenic treasures, and popular sentiment prompted Congress to establish Yellowstone National Park on 1 March 1872. With the passage of the momentous Yellowstone Act, two million acres of public land in Wyoming and Montana were set aside from settlement or sale and dedicated 'as a public park or pleasuring ground for the benefit and enjoyment of the people.' The law also called for the preservation of all the park resources and wonders 'in their natural condition.'

In 1890 Sequoia, General Grant and Yosemite were established as national parks. The establishment of the first national parks reflected a changing attitude about nature among Americans. Because the country was so vast, little thought had been given to the land itself—instead the emphasis was on expansion, for both the land and its resources seemed limitless. This attitude slowly gave way to an appreciation of the beauty and wonder of nature. Some

historians have suggested that the desire to create national parks was fueled by the country's lack of an established identity as a nation. Unlike European countries, the United States did not have a long cultural heritage, but it did have natural wonders that rivaled the cathedrals and castles in the 'old country,' and these wonders were worth preserving for the generations to come.

During the early years of the national parks, a separate movement was under way to protect the cliff dwellings, pueblo ruins and early missions of the Southwest from plunder and destruction. In 1889, Congress authorized the President to set aside the land of the Casa Grande ruin in Arizona, and three years later President Benjamin Harrison established the Casa Grande Reservation.

When Theodore Roosevelt was elected president in 1901, his long-standing interest in natural history furthered the nation's desire to preserve its resources. Roosevelt first came to the Badlands of North Dakota in 1883, and he was so influenced by the time he spent there he would later remark 'I never would have been President if it had not been for my experiences in North Dakota.' Although his initial interests in the area were hunting and ranching, Roosevelt soon grew alarmed by the decimation man had wrought on the large herds of bison that had once roamed the plains. As he watched overgrazing destroy the grasslands and with them the habitats of the songbirds and small mammals, conservation became one of his major concerns, and this desire to protect the environment continued throughout his presidency.

During the Roosevelt administration in 1904, the General Land Office requested an inspection of Indian antiquities in Arizona, New Mexico, Colorado and Utah. Dr Edgar Lee Hewett, the head of the expedition, recommended that certain sites be preserved. His recommendation, along with the help of Representative John F Lacey and Senator Henry Cabot Lodge led to the passage of the Antiquities Act in 1906. The act authorized the President 'to declare by public proclamation historic landmarks, historic and prehistoric structures and other objects of historic or scientific interest' located on federally owned or controlled land to be national monuments. Three months after he signed the Antiquities Act, President Roosevlet declared Devil's Tower in Wyoming the first national monument. Between 1906 and 1978, 12 presidents, using the authority of the Antiquities Act, declared 99 national monuments. Of the 99 national monuments, 27 became or contributed to 24 national parks or national preserves. For example, the Sieur de Monts National Monument in Maine was incorporated into Lafayette National Park in

Left: Early hikers at Glacier National Park in Montana. Even before the park was established in 1910, visitors to the area enjoyed hiking among the rugged splendor of the Rockies.

7

1919. (Lafayette was redesignated Acadia National Park in 1929.)

North of the border, in Canada, similar ideas were brewing. One November morning in 1883, during the construction of the transcontinental Canadian railway, section foreman Frank McCabe and an assistant, William McCardell, discovered a hot spring in the mountains of Alberta. Various people laid claim to the land, but eventually, in 1885, the government intervened and the hot springs were set aside for public use. Using Yellowstone as a model, the Canadian government, on 23 June 1887, established Rocky Mountains Park (later to be known as Banff).

The Rocky Mountains Park Act declared Banff to be 'a public park and pleasure ground for the benefit, education and enjoyment of the people,' and both the government and the Canadian Pacific Railway did much to promote the area as an exclusive spa. Although the act did contain some provisions for protecting the land, only limited conservation measures were taken, largely because the park had little money and manpower to do more. However, attempts were made to reforest the land, to remove logging operations from the park, and to tighten up hunting regulations.

As the century came to a close, additional areas in the Canadian Rockies and Selkirk Mountains were declared park reserves, the first step in becoming a national park. The incomparable beauty of the Lake Louise area was saved from despoliation, the nucleus of parks encompassing the wonders of the Yoho Valley and the snowy Selkirks had been set aside, and the Canadian component of the future Waterton-Glacier International Peace Park had been preserved for posterity. In the early 1900s, concern for the conservation of wildlife led to

the establishment of Elk Island National Park, the first large, federally controlled area to be enclosed as a big game sanctuary. Soon action was taken to establish park reserves in the eastern part of Canada. The first eastern parks—St Lawrence Islands, Point Pelee and Georgian Bay—were carved out of the lands held in trust for the Indians.

The Idea Grows

In 1911, the Rocky Mountain Parks Act, which established Banff, was replaced by the Dominion Forest Reserves and Parks Act. The new act facilitated the establishment of national parks by essentially requiring only a recommendation from the Minister of the Interior to the Governor General in Council. Soon after the act came into being, the Dominion Parks Bureau, under the direction of JB Harkin, was created to administer the national parks. Commissioner Harkin began a program of tourist promotion, combined with wildlife conservation and protection of the environment. Harkin's concern for wildlife is exemplified by the establishment of Wood Buffalo National Park in 1922, a move which is now regarded as one of the most important and far-sighted conservation measures ever taken by the Canadian government. The park, which encompassed the original habitat of wood buffalo, saved the only remaining herd in its native wild state from extinction. Between 1911 and 1945, a protectionist policy was developed which called for the removal of many activities now considered inappropriate for national parks. For example, coal mining regulations were made stricter, and new mines were banned from the parks.

Left: A tourist party at Yosemite National Park in California around the turn of the century.

Above: An excursion to Beaurivage Island in Ontario's St Lawrence Islands National Park in the summer of 1930. The Thousand Islands of the St Lawrence River had been a popular vacation spot since the days following the Civil War, when Americans flocked to the area aboard the railroads' luxurious new Pullman cars.

Far Right: Picnickers on Elk Island, Alberta, circa 1925. Elk Island became a dominion park in 1913 and a national park in 1930.

At about the same time that Canada established its park service, the United States recognized a similar need for better control over its national parks. The early national parks were loosely managed by a variety of different government agencies, from the US Army to the Department of Agriculture. Park enthusiasts called for a unified park management, and on 25 August 1916 — 44 years after Yellowstone National Park was established — President Woodrow Wilson signed legislation creating a new federal bureau, the National Park Service in the Department of the Interior. The new bureau came into being bearing the responsibility for 37 diverse areas.

Between 1916 and 1933, despite World War I and the onset of the Depression, the National Park Service nearly doubled in size. The first park established by the newly created National Park Service was Mount McKinley, authorized in 1917 to protect Dall sheep, caribou, Alaska moose, grizzly bear and other wildlife on or around North America's highest mountain. Two Alaskan National Monuments were also established — Katmai in 1918, the scene of one of the greatest volcanic eruptions of recorded history, and Glacier Bay in 1925, home of 16 great tidewater glaciers and abundant wildlife.

This period also saw the establishment of the first parks east of the Mississippi. The creation of these eastern parks was a significant advance for the system, for it built support in the most densely populated area of the country. Among the parks added during this period were Great Smoky Mountains National Park in the highest section of the Tennessee and North Carolina Appalachians; Shenandoah National Park along the Virginia Blue Ridge, with its spectacular views of the Shenandoah and surrounding countryside; and Mammoth Cave National Park in Kentucky. Because this region of the country did not have vast tracks of unpopulated areas, the eastern parks were not carved out of public domain; instead much land came from private donation. John D Rockefeller Jr made significant contributions of land to form Acadia and Great Smoky Mountains.

Of course, the National Park Service was also establishing parks in the West, including Grand Canyon in Arizona, Bryce Canyon in Utah and Carlsbad Caverns in New Mexico. Two national monuments established during this time — Arches in Utah and Badlands in South Dakota — became national parks in the 1970s.

In the early 1930s both Canada and the United States refined their policies governing their national park systems. Canada passed the National Parks Act in 1930, which stated that the parks were to be left 'unimpaired for the use of future generations.' All industries were to be removed from the parks, and this resulted in boundary changes for some parks. At Banff, for example, the town of Canmore and areas used for lumbering and mining were excised from the park. By this time, Canada's national parks covered 17 areas. Although more emphasis was being placed on conservation, the Dominion Parks Bureau continued its promotion of the parks as Canada's main tourist attraction, a reflection of the policy that the parks were primarily resorts.

In 1933 the National Park Service in the United States underwent a sweeping reorganization when President Franklin D Roosevelt placed all national parks, monuments, military parks, national cemeteries, national memorials, the parks of the National Capital and the Department of Agriculture properties under the administration of the park service. In the 30 years following the reorganization, 93 new units were added to the system, but of these only three entirely new parks were established and four essentially new national parks were formed or expanded from pre-existing holdings.

The first of the new parks was Everglades, which was established in 1934 to protect the largest tropical wilderness in the United States. Until 1980, Everglades was the only national park in the southeastern part of the United States, and it is the only park of its kind. The following year Big Bend National Park was carved out of the wilderness surrounding the Chisos Mountains of southwestern Texas. In 1956, Virgin Islands National Park was established to protect the natural, rugged beauty of St John Island.

In spite of a growing concern and interest in the conservation of natural treasures, some segments of the population were opposed to the establishment of new parks. Olympic National Park, established in 1938, formed its core around Mount Olympus National Monument. Timber companies, however, were adamantly opposed to the park, but the efforts of conservationists, thanks to support from Secretary of the Interior Harold Ickes and President Roosevelt, prevailed.

Below: A vintage photograph of vacationers relaxing at Sol Duc Hot Springs Resort, located in the temperate rain forest of Olympic National Park, Washington.

Above: A 1924 National Geographic party explores the underground world of Carlsbad Caverns in New Mexico. The two men seen here are in King's Palace—829 feet below the earth's surface.

Right: Before its establishment as a national park in 1934, the Great Smoky Mountains were home to a hardy band of settlers. Today, the restored log cabins and barns stand as reminders of those who carved a living from the wilderness of the Appalachian Highlands.

Perhaps the greatest struggle to establish a park centered around Jackson Hole, Wyoming. As early as 1892, Jackson Hole had been considered a possible addition to Yellowstone, and with the establishment of the National Park Service in 1916, the Service and the Interior Department had worked to include Jackson Hole in the system. In 1926, John D Rockefeller Jr visited the area with Horace Albright, superintendent of Yellowstone, and was alarmed to see the view of the Grand Teton Range ruined by unsightly commercial development on private lands. Rockefeller, under the auspices of the Snake River Land Company and with government encouragement, began buying up land, which he then offered to the United States as a gift. Controversy raged when Rockefeller's intent became known. Cattlemen, dude ranchers, packers, hunters, timber interests, local Forest Service officials, local county officials fearing loss of tax revenues, and state leaders unanimously opposed the park. Yielding to the opposition, the state of Wyoming blocked passage of legislation to create a park. Meanwhile, Rockefeller was growing impatient with holding the land and paying taxes on it, so President Roosevelt, under the authority of the Antiquities Act, declared the Jackson Hole National Monument—a consolidation of Rockefeller's land and 179,000 acres from the Teton National Forest adjacent to Grand Teton National Park.

Wyoming's politicians, most notably Representative Frank A Barrett, were outraged by Roosevelt's action. Barrett and others introduced bills to abolish the monument as well as the proclamation authority provided by the Antiquities Act. In 1944 Congress passed legislation abolishing the monument, but it was vetoed by Roosevelt. The debate was settled happily, if belatedly, in 1950, when legislation signed by Harry Truman created a new Grand Teton National Park of 298,000 acres by consolidating the monument with the old Grand Teton National Park. The legislation also included special provisions for tax revenue compensation and hunting, and it prohibited establishing or enlarging national parks and monuments in Wyoming, except by congressional authorization. Although restricted to Wyoming, the legislation effectively ceased the presidential proclamation of large scientific national monuments throughout the United States. In the 35 years following the Jackson Hole controversy, only two more national monuments were so established: Buck Island Reef in the Virgin Islands and Marble Canyon in Arizona.

National Parks Today

The 1960s saw a dawning of an age of expansion, coupled with an increased concern for conservation and preservation, for national parks. In the United States, from 1964 to 1972, under the guidance of Director George B Hartzog, the National Park System established five new national parks and upgraded two national monuments to parks. Secretary of the Interior Stewart L Udall backed this expansion, while encouraging the perpetuation and restoration of the parks. Between 1978 and 1980, the total land more than doubled with the acquisition of the Alaskan parklands—America's last true wilderness.

In Canada, a major milestone was passed with the 1964 policy statement, which marked a drastic change in attitude. Previous park policy had emphasized the resort aspect of the parks; now more emphasis was placed on ecology. The new policy also dealt specifically with such issues as transportation and ski areas. Further changes in policy were shaped by the public hearing process. The strength and influence of public input was clearly illustrated in 1972 by the decision to shelve large-scale development plans at Lake Louise. The present policy reflects the goal of the Canadian government to represent the diversity of landscapes and wildlife within each of the country's provinces and territories.

Today, national parks exist from the Everglades in southern Florida to the far north reaches of Ellesmere Island in the Arctic, from the Hawaiian Islands in the Pacific Ocean to Newfoundland's eastern shore.

Left: Captain Daniel C Kingman's camp at Mammoth Hot Springs in Yellowstone National Park in 1886. Established in 1872, Yellowstone was the world's first national park.

Right: The first automobile to go through Yellowstone, at Old Faithful Inn in 1915.

Below. Old Faithful Inn in 1912. Having survived a close call with the catastrophic forest fires of 1988, the Inn is still providing fine accommodations today. It is located adjacent to Old Faithful Geyser—the world's best known geyser.

THE MARITIMES

Cape Breton Highlands, Nova Scotia

Established: 1936   Acreage: 234,880

Although separated from the mainland of Nova Scotia by the Strait of Canso, Cape Breton Island is easily accessible from the mainland by causeway. The picturesque coastline is broken by bays and inlets. Rising abruptly from the water are rugged hills and mountains which sweep back to form a broad plateau, the dominant feature of the park. From the ocean, panoramas of hillside, cliff, bay and valley are seen; and from the land, vistas of sandy cove, rocky cape and jagged, tide-worn rocks, against the blue background of the Atlantic Ocean or the Gulf of St Lawrence.

White-tailed deer, bobcat, red fox, black bear, woodland jumping mouse, red-backed vole and masked shrew are among the mammals that inhabit the deciduous and mixed forests of the lowland coastal fringes and valleys. Snowshoe hare, red squirrel and moose are typical species found in the boreal highlands, which cover over half the land surface of the park. The highlands, the largest remaining wilderness in Nova Scotia, is one of the last refuges in the Maritimes for Canada lynx and pine marten.

Over-hunting and disease wiped out the moose and wood-land caribou by the early 1900s, but moose were successfully reintroduced into the park in 1947 and 1948 from stock from Alberta.

During the summer, harbor porpoise, harbor seal and pilot, finback and minke whales are frequently seen in the waters surrounding the island. Many species of birds can be seen in the park, including red-eyed vireo, blue jay, white-throated sparrow, hermit thrush, spruce grouse, merlin, great horned owl, arctic terns and 18 species of warblers.

Cape Breton National Park offers both summer and winter recreation activities. Summer visitors can hike on the many trails, play golf or tennis, fish for trout and salmon and swim in both fresh and salt water. The famous Cabot Trail, one of Canada's most popular scenic drives, winds through the park. The northern part of the park is in a snow belt. Snowshoeing, cross country skiing, skating and beautiful star-studded winter nights beside the sea are all part of the fun.

The early history of Cape Breton Island is clouded and inconclusive. When Cape Breton was ceded by England to France after the Treaty of Utrecht in 1713, the walled city and fortress of Louisbourg were built, around which revolved a long struggle for supremacy in North America. French rule ended in Canada with the capture of Quebec in 1759. Settlement of parts of the island by Acadians from Nova Scotia was followed by Scottish immigration. Descendents of these early pioneers still constitute a large number of the island's present population.

*Previous pages: Covehead Lighthouse in Prince Edward Island stands watch over the shore. In days past, the eastern coast of Canada was the scene of many shipwrecks. Among the ships lost was the famous **Marco Polo**, which foundered off Cape Cavendish in August 1883.*

Right: The famed Cabot Trail winds through Cape Breton Highlands National Park. Pictured on the left is Corney Brook campground on the Gulf of St Lawrence.

Below: Winter time fun at Cape Breton Highlands includes cross country skiing in the Clyburn Valley.

Forillon, Quebec

Established: 1970   Acreage: 59,392

Forillon National Park occupies much of the eastern part of Cap Gaspé known as the Forillon Peninsula. The word 'Gaspé' is probably an Indian word meaning land's end. It refers to the prominent, rocky cape—the first land seen on approaching the Gulf of St Lawrence from the southeast. Long before the creation of the park, the Gaspé region was a popular tourist destination. In the 1920s the Perron Boulevard (now Highway 132) afforded a magnificent drive. For most of the route, the road skirts the St Lawrence River and the gulf, passes picturesque fishing villages, climbs steep grades and descends to coves with sandy beaches. East, the almost vertical limestone cliffs of Forillon Peninsula rise from the sea. A complete tour of the Gaspé Peninsula, a trip of about 550 miles (885 kilometers), is one the most spectacular drives in eastern Canada.

Little was known of the Gulf of St Lawrence and the Gaspé region before Jacques Cartier's first voyage to North America in 1534, although archeological investigations have revealed human habitation centuries before Cartier arrived. It is likely that groups of hunters migrated from the south and west to the Gaspé territory 10,000 years ago and lived by hunting caribou, catching fish and gathering wild fruit.

Early Europeans had hoped to trade in furs as well as fish, but the abundance of cod, redfish and herring led to its dominance in the area's economy. Petit-Gaspé, one of the oldest of the former fishing communities on the bay, has long been a tourist attraction. The original settlers came from the British Channel Islands, and St Peter's Anglican Church is one of its showpieces. At Grande-Grève, an original Gaspé settlement has been recreated that includes restored houses, commercial buildings and other village structures. These allow visitors to examine the self-sufficient lifestyle of the farmer-fishermen, the cod fishing business, the monopoly of the trading company in the area, and the physical environment and social organizations of the settlement. Visitors to the park can also enjoy boat excursions, hiking, picnicking and, in winter, skiing.

Far left: From the vantage point of Cape Bon Ami in Forillon National Park, one has a view of both the Gulf of St Lawrence and the Bay of Gaspé.

*Wildlife in the park includes the red squirrel (**below left**) and the red fox (**below**).*

Fundy, New Brunswick

Established: 1948   Acreage: 50,880

The word 'Fundy' was originally believed to come from the Portuguese 'fondo,' meaning deep. Later research decided that the name was an English corruption of the French word 'fendu,' or split. No matter what the origin of the name, the Bay of Fundy, which separates the provinces of New Brunswick and Nova Scotia, is remarkable for its tremendous tides, believed to be the highest in the world—spring tides reach a height of 59 to 68 feet.

Inland, the park consists of rolling forested land, dotted with small lakes, many of which provide the source of streams which feed its main rivers, the Upper Salmon and the Point Wolfe. High swift tides, aided by wind and wave action, have carved and sculptured the rugged shoreline into sheltered coves and bold promontories. The rugged coastline provides a stark contrast to the sylvan solitude of the wood-

lands. The forests, which combine broad-leaved with evergreen trees, present a dazzling array of color in the autumn as the gold and crimson of the deciduous species mingle with the dark green of the conifers.

The earliest visitors to the Bay of Fundy were Sieur de Monts and Samuel de Champlain, who entered the mouth of the St John River in 1604. Permanent settlement of the lands north of the bay did not occur until the arrival of the United Empire Loyalists in 1783. Lumbering became the main industry, and employed many residents for more than 100 years. During the peak years of the lumber trade, three- and four-masted schooners were loaded from wharves at Point Wolfe and Alma, and larger vessels were loaded offshore from barges. Small cemeteries, dams and picturesque covered bridges remind today's visitors of the former inhabitants.

Today, visitors to the park enjoy camping, hiking and fishing. The park's variety of topographical features—forests, meadows and coastline—creates an ideal environment for nature study. Fundy boasts a wealth of wildflowers, over 200 hundred varieties, and 77 species of birds.

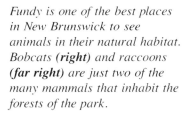

Fundy is one of the best places in New Brunswick to see animals in their natural habitat. Bobcats (right) and raccoons (far right) are just two of the many mammals that inhabit the forests of the park.

Below: *Hiking the Moosehorn Trail along the rocky Upper Salmon River.*

Gros Morne, Newfoundland

Established: 1970   Acreage: 480,000

Gros Morne National Park contains strikingly different geological features—from mountains and cliffs, to waterfalls and lakes, to bogs and sand dunes. These fabulous geological features have earned the park international recognition as one of the world's most outstanding natural areas. Most of the landscape was created by continental drift, including the intriguing Tablelands—a piece of the earth's interior that has been forced to the surface. Found in the eastern section of the park, the Long Range Mountains comprise roughly 42 percent of the total area of Gros Morne. The mountains were formed through the erosion of massive uplifted and tilted coastal blocks. From a distance the mountains appear flat, but in reality they consist of a series of ridges and wide valleys separated by low bluffs. Weather varies greatly in the Long Range area. A day of fog, sleet and gale force winds may be followed by one of bright sunshine. In winter, abundant snowfall provides the opportunity for cross country skiing, snowshoeing and winter camping.

Each area of the park has its own plants and animals. Along the coastline are volcanic sea stacks and caves, headlands, sand and cobblestone beaches and dunes, as well as periwinkles and sea urchins. Moose, woodland caribou, fox, lynx, beaver and snowshoe hare are among the mammals that make their home in the park. The ponds and streams of the park are filled with trout and salmon, and off-shore waters abound with cod, sea perch, mackerel, and sea trout.

Hiking on one of the park's many trails offers the best way to explore the varied scenery of Gros Morne. Trails lead through the tuckamore—tangled, twisted spruce trees—to sights of incredible fiords and waterfalls. The park also has a rich cultural heritage, still evident in the lifestyle of the local communities. For thousands of years, residents of the area have built their lives around fishing.

Right: A hiker takes a brief respite in the peaceful woods along the Southeast Brook.

Below: Gros Morne is a study in contrasting landscapes. Here a lone hiker perches high amid the rugged, mountainous terrain of Gros Morne. Not far away lie beaches and sanddunes.

Kejimkujik, Nova Scotia

Established: 1968   Acreage: 94,272

In contrast to the maritime character of Cape Breton Highlands National Park, Kejimkujik National Park forms an excellent example of inland Nova Scotia. The park is a land of numerous lakes—many of them dotted with islands—of tumbling streams, and of rocky landscapes with a background of coniferous and hardwood forests. The park gets its name from the largest lake within its boundaries, Kejimkujik, a Micmac Indian word which is thought to mean 'the stricture passage,' referring to the fish weirs that backed up the water and caused the lake to 'swell.'

Much of the park was sculptured by the last Ice Age. Thick glaciers and sheets of ice then covered the area, scouring the rocky outcrops and gouging out depressions which now contain shallow lakes. After the climate warmed up and the ice melted, huge granite boulders carried along by the ice were left scattered across the land or in the lakes. The layer of soil left behind after the retreat of the ice is thin and rocky. In the eastern part of the park, where the soil has more depth, it was pushed into dome-shaped or elongated hills known as drumlins.

Much of the area was once the home of the Micmac Indians, whose petroglyphs can be found on the slate outcrops along the shores of Kejimkujik Lake. These sketches, representing animals such as moose and caribou, hunting and fishing techniques and Micmac women's headgear, are prominent at the entrance to Fairy Bay, at Peter Point and at George Lake.

Kouchibouguac, New Brunswick

Established: 1969   Acreage: 55,680

Located on the Kouchibouguac Bay along the northern section of the Northumberland Strait, the park's most outstanding natural feature is the 15-mile sweep of offshore sandbars which stretch across its entire ocean front. Behind this ribbon of dunes are quiet lagoons and bays that provide excellent protected swimming and boating.

The park's inland plain is cut by streams and rivers, and has both forested regions and large areas of salt and fresh water bogs and marshes. Plant life in the park ranges from the stunted trees, Labrador tea, pitcher plant and blueberry bush of the wetlands to the black and red spruce, pine and balsam fir of the forests.

Black bear, bobcat, white-tailed deer, moose, fox and squirrel are common, and birdlife includes swamp, field, woodland and shore species. Sandpiper wood duck, common eider, ruffed grouse, raven, gull and heron inhabit the park. Every autumn and spring migratory waterfowl touch down here to feed and rest. The rivers, streams and ocean waters of the park are inhabited by a wide variety of shellfish and fresh and salt water fish, including lake trout, whitefish, herring, bass, salmon and lobster.

Right: For many, the serene coastline of Kouchibouguac provides a welcome escape from the hectic pace of urban life.

Below: Tern Island in Kouchibouguac National Park is home to one of the largest tern nesting sites in North America.

Mingan Archipelago, Quebec

Established: 1984   Acreage: 23,880

The Mingan Archipelago contains some 40 islands in a narrow band in the Gulf of St Lawrence, east of Sept-Îles and north of Anticosti Island. The islands are a unique land of fragile beauty, with unusual rock pillars sculpted by the wind and sea and rare plants and flowers found nowhere else in Canada. Puffins and other seabirds nest on these limestone isles, while porpoises, seals and whales feed in the fertile offshore waters.

Visitors to the Mingan Archipelago can enjoy guided water tours, primitive camping, and boating—on a charter or on their own boat. There are no facilities within the park reserve; visitor centers are located on the mainland in Havre-St-Pierre and nearby villages.

The islands of the Mingan Archipelago are inhabited by a variety of seabirds, including puffins (right).

***Far right:** Seals splash about the protected waters of the Mingan Archipelago in the Gulf of St Lawrence.*

***Below:** The forces of wind and water have carved these strangely shaped pillars of rock.*

Prince Edward Island, Prince Edward Island

Established: 1937   Acreage: 4480

Encompassing a coastline strip extending nearly 25 miles along the north shore of the island, Prince Edward Island National Park includes some of the finest saltwater beaches in Canada. Reddish in color and beaten smooth and broad by the surf, they permit swimming in water that is warmer than at many points along the Atlantic coast to the south. Landward from the beaches, sand dunes and red sandstone cliffs rise to considerable heights.

The written history of Prince Edward Island dates back to the sixteenth century. Jacques Cartier sailed along the north shores of the island and made some landings on his first voyage in 1534. But long before Cartier arrived, the island was inhabited by the Micmac Indians, who called it 'Epagwit,' meaning resting on the waves. The island was later settled first by emigrants from France, and then by Acadians. Since the early days of settlement, many residents of the province have gained a livelihood from agriculture and by fishing the waters of the Gulf of St Lawrence. Small fleets of fishing boats still operate from their home ports in the picturesque villages that lie within the bays and inlets.

Included in the park are Dalvay by the Sea and Green Gables. Dalvay by the Sea, known as Dalvay House, represents a splendid example of the large summer homes erected by opulent citizens in an era when costs were low and income taxes were nonexistent. Long before it was incorporated in the park, Green Gables had become a point of interest in the Cavendish area. The farmhouse, erected around the mid-1850s, had a literary connection with the novels of Lucy Maud Montgomery. Since the publication of *Anne of Green Gables* in 1908, the white farmhouse, trimmed in green, has attracted visitors.

Below: *Cape Turner on Prince Edward Island. Every July and August the warm salt water beaches of the park draw thousands of vacationers.*

Terra Nova, Newfoundland

Established: 1957   Acreage: 97,987

Terra Nova, or 'new land,' is Canada's most easterly park and was created to represent the Atlantic Uplands of the eastern portion of Newfoundland and to protect remnants of the ancient Appalachian Mountains. Thirty percent of the park is ocean water. Three tongues of Bonavista Bay indent the land—Southwest Arm (Alexander Bay), Newman Sound and Clode Sound. The land was shaped by the glaciers during the Ice Age, and the resulting rock formations, deposits of sand, gravel and large boulders, and the fiords along the coast are among the park's distinctive features.

The region owes its temperate climate to the sea. The warm Gulf Stream flowing past Newfoundland delays and moderates the onset of winter, while Labrador Current brings with it pack ice and enormous icebergs from the glaciers of Greenland and the polar cap. In turn, the moderate climate of Terra Nova affects the area's plants and animals. The rolling hills are cloaked in the greens and greys of black spruce and balsam fir. Stands of white birch and poplar are found throughout the park, interspersed by alder and red maple in the stream valleys. Bogs filled with moss, bog laurel, leatherleaf, pitcher plant and Labrador tea are abundant, but wildlife is somewhat limited, owing to the isolation of Newfoundland from the Canadian mainland.

Most reminders of Terra Nova's cultural heritage lie along the coast. Europeans reached the area as early as the 1500s. Explorers, fishermen and pirates travelled this coast, taking refuge and settling in the many hidden caves and harbors. The use of timber for boat building developed into a major lumber industry, and in fact some mills were operating until the land was acquired for the parks in the late 1950s.

*Snowshoe hare (**far right, top**) were introduced to Terra Nova by humans in the nineteenth century, but are now as plentiful as the native lynx, bear and beaver (**far right, bottom**).*

Below: The Great Horned Owl, the largest and most familiar owl, is a common part of the 'night life' of the Maritimes.

Above: Fishing for salmon along the scenic Northwest River. Terra Nova is a fisherman's dream come true.

Because the ocean separates Newfoundland from the rest of Canada, the animals have thus evolved somewhat differently from those found on the mainland. For example, the moose (**right**) are smaller than their mainland brothers.

THE
NORTHEAST

Acadia, Maine

Established: 1916   Acreage: 39,114

Acadia National Park, located on Mount Desert Island off the coast of Maine, was created to preserve the rugged beauty of the New England coastline. Its surf-splashed shores rise to the highest elevation along the Atlantic coast. Cadillac Mountain, elevation 1530 feet (466 meters) and Mount Sargeant at 1373 feet (418 meters) are its highest points. More than 275 species of birds inhabit the park.

Abnaki Indians knew Mount Desert Island as 'the sloping land' thousands of years before the white man landed on the rugged Maine coast. In 1604 France's Samuel de Champlain made the first important contribution to the historical record of the island by naming it Mount Desert Island, after its bare and rocky mountain summits.

By the early 1800s, farming and lumbering vied with fishing and shipbuilding as major occupations, and the familiar sights of fishermen and sailors, fish racks and shipyards, revealed a way of life and a breed of people linked to the sea.

It was the outsiders—artists and journalists—who proclaimed the beauties of this area to the world in the mid-1800s. People flocked to Acadia to enjoy its scenery, undaunted by crude accommodations and simple food, and soon tourism quickly became a major industry. Affluent citizens such as the Rockefellers, Morgans, Fords, Carnegies and Vanderbilts chose to summer here.

Although the wealthy of the early twentieth century came primarily to play, they had much to do with preserving the landscape we know today. George B Dorr devoted his life and fortune to Acadia and became the park's first superintendent. John D Rockefeller Jr built 57 miles of carriage paths between 1915 and 1933 and donated more than 11,000 acres, nearly one-third of the park's area. Acadia is unique because it was neither carved out of public lands nor bought with public funds. The park was envisioned and donated through the efforts of private citizens. George Dorr offered the land to the federal government, and in 1916 President Wilson announced the creation of Sieur de Monts National Monument. Three years later it became Lafayette National Park, the first national park east of the Mississippi. In 1929, the name was changed to Acadia.

Right: The top of Cadillac Mountain—the highest point in Acadia—offers a stunning view of the rocky New England Coast.

Facing page, top: Land and sea meet at Acadia National Park, and between the sea and the forested mountains lies the tidal zone—a world brimming with life forms that a poet once mused 'belong to neither land nor sea'.

Previous pages: Canoers on glistening Lake Francais in La Mauricie National Park in Quebec. Canoeing is a popular activity on the park's numerous lakes.

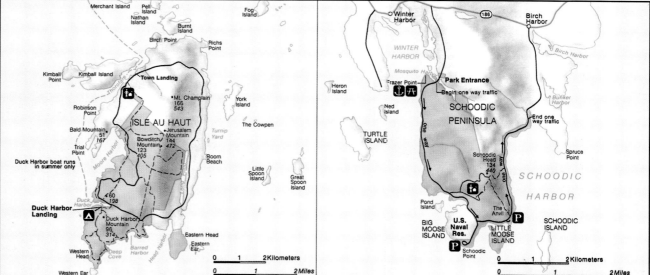

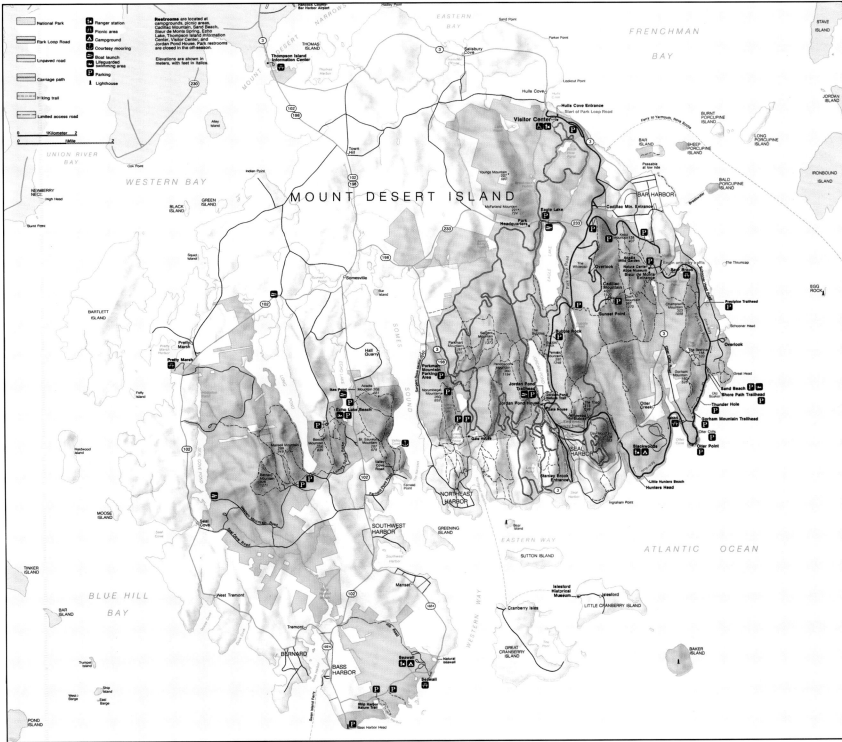

Above: *Frolicking in the surf at sunny Sand Beach in Acadia. The beach is the only swimming area within the park.*

Left: *Herring gulls are just one of the 300 species of birds seen in Acadia. The gulls often follow fishing boats, squawking loudly—and persistently—for scraps.*

Far left: *Around the turn of the century the affluent were drawn to the rugged beauty of Otter Cliffs. Though they came to relax, their interest in the island led to efforts to preserve the landscape for us today.*

Bruce Peninsula, Ontario

Established: 1988   Acreage: 66,739

The story of prehistoric Ontario is revealed in the rocks and landforms of Bruce Peninsula, a finger of limestone separating Georgian Bay from the main basin of Lake Huron. At the peninsula's tip lies the Bruce Peninsula National Park, an area of limestone cliffs, mixed woodlots, abundant wetlands and tranquil beaches. At one time the park area was covered by a glacier, which scraped away the topsoil, scratched the rocks and littered the area with boulders transported from the north.

The park is dominated by the spectacular Niagara Escarpment. Marked by a rugged wall of limestone, the escarpment

crosses southern Ontario, heads up the Georgian Bay side of the peninsula, and submerges in the bay, reappearing as islands. In the park, this rough tableland of limestone meets the Georgian Bay in cliffs and cobblestone beaches, forming the park's eastern boundary. The Niagara Escarpment originated four million years ago in the remains of coral and other creatures that built up, forming limestone, on the shallow sea. As the weak layers beneath the limestone began to erode, large sections of limestone broke off, forming the escarpment.

Despite a fire in the late 1800s that decimated the original forest, 'the Bruce' is a botanist's paradise. The park is covered with a mixed and often dense forest of cedar, balsam, fir, spruce, birch and aspen, and has over 40 species of orchids, 20 species of ferns and five species of insectivorous plants.

Over 100 species of birds, as well as deer, snowshoe hare, red squirrel, beaver, chipmunk and fox are regularly seen in the park. The Bruce is also a haven for the rare Massaguaga rattlesnake. Ontario's best known hiking trail—the Bruce Trail—is in the park.

The park area encompasses Fathom Five National Marine Park, Canada's first national *marine* park. Fathom Five includes the treacherous waters of the Cape Hurd Islands area at the tip of the Bruce Peninsula. One of the best known of the islands is Flowerpot Island, a large and distinctive island that derives its name from large limestone pillars formed by the erosion of the adjacent cliffs on the southeastern shore. Growths of bushes and plants on the tops and in crevices of the columns have accentuated their resemblance to flowerpots. According to the local folklore, the caves and flowerpots of this beautiful island were shrouded in ancient taboos. Today, however, the island is known for its walking trails, picnic areas, rare orchids and, of course, its flowerpot rock formations.

Right: The treacherous waters at the tip of Bruce Peninsula once claimed many ships. Today, scuba divers explore the remains of these vessels.

Below: To the native population, Flowerpot Island—named for the distinctive shape of the rock pillars—was once a land cloaked in taboos and mystery.

Georgian Bay Islands, Ontario

Established: 1929   Acreage: 3500

Since the early days of the twentieth century, the Georgian Bay region has served as a holiday resort. Its cool blue waters, jutting capes and a variety of picturesque islands have combined to attract campers, boaters, fishermen and artists. Nature was lavish in the provision of islands, which form an archipelago believed to contain at least 30,000 units.

For many thousands of years, people have been drawn to Georgian Bay. The first peoples may have lived here over 10,000 years ago, hunting and gathering. In the early seventeenth century, the area was occupied by the Ojibwa in the north and east, the Huron in the south and the Petun on the Bruce Peninsula. The Ojibwa fished and hunted, while the Huron and Peton farmed. As European cultures moved into the area, the focus moved away from major food sources to the development of trade routes on Georgian Bay. Voyageur canoes plied the waters from the head of Lake Superior with furs destined for Montreal. The sheltered routes through Georgian Bay offered many advantages over the open water of Lake Huron and Lake Erie.

The famous Canadian Group of Seven captured the beauty of the area in many of their paintings. The hard granite and gneiss rock of these islands has changed little over the past 8000 years. Today, Georgian Bay Islands National Park is in the heart of Canada's vacationland. The islands offer many recreational activities—camping, picnicking and hiking—and visitors can enjoy swimming, snorkeling, scuba diving, swimming, boating and fishing in the surrounding waters.

Far left: The rocky beaches and windswept pines have long attracted people to the islands of the Georgian Bay. The park, which is accessible only by boat, is composed of 59 islands or parts of islands.

Below: Sunset on the bay marks the end of a pleasurable day exploring the coastal waters.

A rugged landscape of glacier-scraped rocks dominates the northern islands of Georgian Bay Islands National Park, providing a stark contrast to the rich hardwood forests of the southern areas of the park.

Isle Royale, Michigan

Established: 1931   Acreage: 571,790

In Lake Superior's northwest corner sits a wilderness archipelago, a roadless land of unspoiled forests, refreshing lakes, rugged scenic shores and wild creatures—accessible only by boat or floatplane. Isle Royale has magnificent forests of aspen, white and yellow birch, balsam fir, northern white cedar, and white and black spruce. Many wildflowers are found on the island, including over 32 species of orchids. Foot trails cover 166 miles (267 km) on Isle Royale, and the island contains numerous inland lakes.

The island supports wolves and moose, both of which probably crossed the ice from Canada in the early part of this century. Part of the island's uniqueness lies in its complex, yet simple, system of natural processes, a system in which moose are dependent on both wolves and beaver—wolves to control the population and beaver to build dams that foster the growth of vegetation upon which the moose feed. For a time the policy was to control the wolf population. This was overdone to such an extent that the deer and moose multiplied to a dangerous number, and they overbrowsed their natural range to a point of mass starvation. Other wild animals on Isle Royale are deer, fox, beaver, mink and snowshoe rabbits.

Long before Europeans saw Isle Royale, Indians mined copper here. On the Store Trail out toward Scoville Point one passes three small pits in the rock which indicate mining activity. Using rounded beach stones as hammers to pound the copper out of the hard bedrock, they formed the copper into beads, fishhooks, knives and other objects. By the 1840s, the only evidence of Indian activity were the remains of a maple sugaring camp on Sugar Mountain and a seasonal fishing camp on Grace Island. Commercial fishing began on Isle Royale in 1837 with the American Fur Company's fishing posts. The major economic species were lake trout, whitefish and herring. Today there are three active fisheries on the island using handlifted gill nets. Sport fishing has replaced commercial fishing, with lake, brook and rainbow trout; northern pike; walleye; and northern pike the most sought after species. Fishing is good throughout the season, but spring and fall produce the largest catches.

Above right, top: At the turn of the century, there were no wolves on Isle Royale. Today, however, they play an important part in the ecology of the island by controlling the moose population. Wolves are highly intelligent and social animals that form extremely organized packs. Every individual, from the dominant pair to the weakest pup, has a specific place in the pack hierarchy.

Above right, middle: In the spring and summer, the island teems with wildflowers.

Right: Fishing has always been good in the cold waters of Lake Superior off Isle Royale. Even before 1800, commercial fishing was a mainstay of the island's economy; today, however, sport fishing has supplanted commercial fishing.

Facing page, top: Among Isle Royale's backcountry values are its natural sights and sounds. Hiking is perhaps the best way to enjoy the wild solitude of the park.

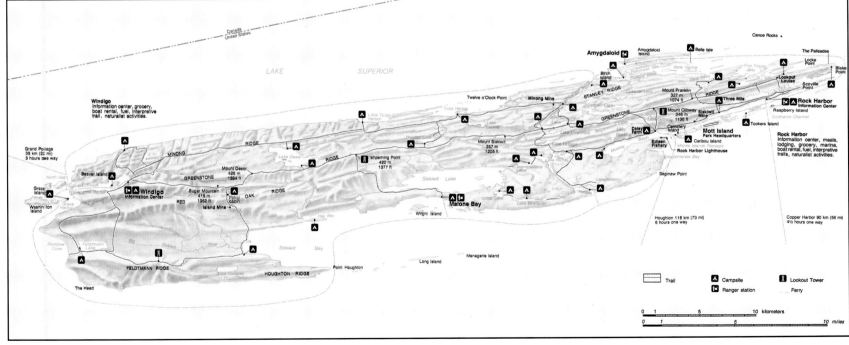

La Mauricie, Quebec

Established: 1970   Acreage: 166,309

Lying near Shawinigan and Grand Mère, barely two hours by car from Montreal and Quebec City, La Mauricie National Park was established to illustrate a feature of the Canadian Shield, to which the Great Lakes-St Lawrence Precambrian Region belongs. Probably the most well-known feature in the park is the Wapizagonke-Antikagamac Passage. Ever since it was formed about a billion years ago as a fracture in the earth's crust, the passage has served as a corridor, giving the area a long and varied history.

Eighty thousand years ago, mammoths and giant cervidae crossed over from Asia to North America via the Bering Strait, which was then dry. In their pursuit was a relentless predator—man. During this time a thick ice cap covered almost all of this continent, leaving only a narrow corridor leading to the south through which both beast and man travelled. Twenty thousand years ago the North American glacier receded, leaving behind it the Laurentian Mountains, polished, riddled with basins and cut with valleys that retained the meltwater. Over thousands of years, wildlife spread and the human population increased.

More recently the Mauricie has been the home of numerous Amerindians peoples—Crees, Algonquins, Iroquois and Attikameks—who hunted, gathered and farmed. By the 1700s plentiful wild game meant furs, a precious commodity that was fashionable in Europe. After the English conquest in 1760 men entered the forests for timber. Oddly, it was Napoleon Bonaparte who sparked the exploitation of the Quebec forests. Intent on conquering Europe, the French Empire cut off timber supplies to England, which then had to look to its colonies in Canada and invest the capital to develop the local industry. Quebec soon became a thriving port and shipbuilding center. Today, the Wapizagonke-Antikagamac Passage provides endless delight for fishermen, canoers, campers and cross country skiers.

Far Right: La Mauricie's Waber Falls, 120 feet high, are well worth the canoe trip or hike necessary to visit them.

Below: The cliffs on Lake Anticagamac. The lakes, streams and waterfalls of the park are scattered amid rounded hills and lush forests.

Point Pelee, Ontario

Established: 1918   Acreage: 3840

Point Pelee, one of Canada's smallest national parks, resembles an inverted triangle, pointing southerly, like a long finger into the western end of Lake Erie. It is also an unusual park—it is a sandpit. Ten thousand years ago, glaciers deposited a ridge of gravel across Lake Erie. Sands eroded from the north shore of the lake were swept onto this base and formed Point Pelee, which owes its name to the French word 'Pelee,' meaning bare, presumably from the long treeless spit that forms the tip.

Although the marsh dominates the park, Point Pelee has a fascinating blend of forest, fields and beach. Spreading across two-thirds of the park, the marsh is a jigsaw arrangement of cattails and ponds. The remaining third of the park was at one time a dense southern forest, whose unusually large variety of trees included the hackberry, sassafras, sycamore, black walnut, honey-locust and blue ash. Surrounding the marsh and forest is a necklace of sand and pebble beach. This mix of marsh, forest, field and beach, combined with Pelee's location, attracts thousands of birds on their biannual migrations.

In 1799, the British declared the southern portion of the Point Pelee peninsula a naval reserve, establishing the basis for today's park boundaries. Over the next hundred years, squatters cleared areas for farming, trapped and hunted the marsh and established commercial fisheries on the lake. By 1900, a handful of naturalists recognized the area as an important stopover site for migrating birds. Point Pelee was the first park in Canada to be created on the merit of its biological value.

Below: The Marsh Boardwalk, a circular trail through Point Pelee, reaches into a sea of cattails and along the edge of ponds. Because the park is small, walking is an ideal way to explore it.

Pukaskwa, Ontario

Established: 1978   Acreage: 464,000

Along the northeast shore of Lake Superior there is no place more inaccessible than Pukaskwa (pronounced puck-a-saw). Called 'the wild shore of an inland sea,' Pukaskwa National Park is located where the Canadian Shield (the wild shore) meets the northeast shore of Lake Superior (the inland sea) on the southern edge of Ontario's boreal forests.

The terrain is hilly, broken by ridges and cliffs and riddled with rock-rimmed lakes. In this wilderness live the moose, wolf, black bear and woodland caribou. The interior is well-forested, with spruce, fir and cedar mixed with birch and aspen. The Coastal Hiking Trail winds from Hattie Cove, south through boreal forest and over the hummocky rock of the Shield to the North Swallow River.

As recently as the 1930s, Pukaskwa's hills and swamps were alive with lumberjacks. Logging started at Pukaskwa around 1905. During the winter the only link with the world was the two dog teams that carried mail over the 70 pathless miles from the railway town of White River. Today only memories and vintage cabins recall the once thriving logging industry.

Far right: The rugged trails through Pukasawa are clearly not for the faint of heart.

Below: White water adventure awaits one on the White River. The trip can be made alone or with a guide.

St Lawrence Islands, Ontario

Established: 1914   Acreage: 1250

Long before written history, early North Americans believed that petals of heavenly flowers fell to earth and were scattered on the mighty river, creating the Thousand Islands, the Garden of the Great Spirit. Today, part of this garden has become Canada's smallest national park—St Lawrence Islands.

A short walk across an island can take one from a northern coniferous forest to a stand of southern hardwood. Hot, dry southwest slopes, exposed to sun and wind, create a climate typical of latitudes much further south. In contrast, protected northeast slopes are cool, moist and shaded. This phenomenon, called 'microclimate,' maintains the islands' remarkable variety of flora and fauna. The pitch pine—the park's symbol—flourishes here, along with the wild turkey and the nonpoisonous black rat snake.

For plants and animals, the granite domes of the Thousand Islands present a timeless challenge which has been no less real for man. Indians, explorers, fur traders and missionaries witnessed the subtle beauty of the Thousand Islands while seeking the adventure of a new land. In 1812, at the outbreak of war between Britain and the United States, settlers found themselves on the country's most vital water route. The St Lawrence was the only route for guns, ammunition and supplies. The railways built after the American Civil War brought many tourists, transforming the Thousand Islands into one of the earliest recreational areas in Canada.

Far right: Many rare plants and animals are found in St Lawrence Islands National Park, among them the striking pitch pine—the park's symbol.

Below: Visitors to the St Lawrence Islands can enjoy the solitude of an afternoon spent canoeing the waters of the park.

Right: Fishing from a skiff is an enjoyable way to spend a warm summer day.

Far right: Boating has always been a popular summer activity in the waters of the Thousand Islands. Before the era of accurate navigational charts, the St Lawrence was renowned for its dangerous shoals.

Right: The delicate and rare rue anemone is seldom seen outside of St Lawrence Islands National Park.

Below: The sharp-shinned hawk, one of the smallest in the hawk family, makes its home in the park.

Voyageurs, Minnesota

Established: 1971   Acreage: 219,128

Water dominates the Voyageur National Park landscape. Within its boundaries more than 30 lakes fill glacier-carved rock basins. Between these lakes and adjacent rocky knobs and ridges extend bogs, marshes and beaver ponds. Upon arriving at one of the park's four entrances, the visitor leaves his car behind, and sets out by water much as the voyageurs travelled in the heyday of the fur trade in the late eighteenth and early nineteenth centuries. Boat trips are available on Rainy, Kabetogama and Crane lakes and on Ash River.

As the fur trade expanded westward, it depended heavily upon the voyageurs, or French-Canadian canoemen, who moved the pelts and trade goods between Montreal and the Canadian Northwest. The route of these adventurers, who frequently paddled 16 hours a day, became so established that the 1783 treaty ending the American Revolution specified that the international boundary should follow their 'customary waterway' between Lake Superior and Lake of the Woods. Today, the park adjoins a 56-mile stretch of that voyageurs' highway.

Look out across the landscape here and you will notice the elements of the fur trade itself. The water provided the highway, fur-bearing animals provided the goods, and the endless forests furnished the materials for the birch-bark canoes. Nature's abundance is evident in other ways here. The park is in the heart of the only region in the continental United States where the eastern timber wolf survives. Other wild animals include moose, deer and black bear.

Facing page, top: The peaceful waters of Anderson Bay were once traversed by the voyageurs—the French-Canadian trappers of the seventeenth and eighteenth centuries.

Facing page, bottom: The waterways of the park can be enjoyed either by canoe or motorboat. In the winter, the waters freeze, but the snow blankets land and lake and skiing becomes the dominant mode of travel.

Right: The lakes of Voyageurs National Park are interspersed with forests of cedar, spruce and birch.

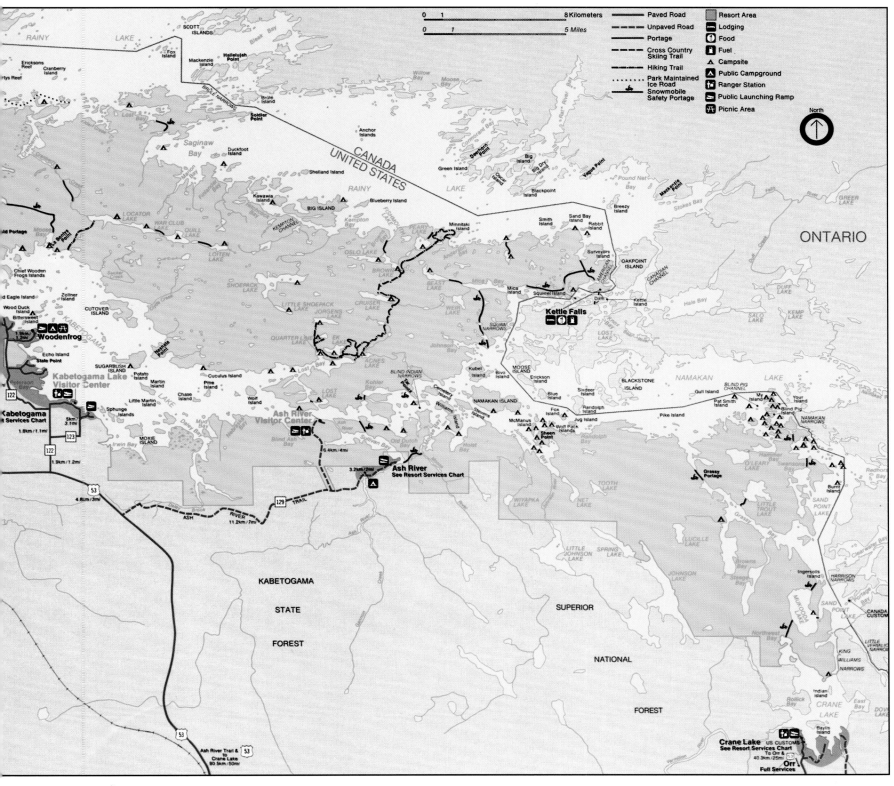

THE SOUTHEAST

Biscayne, Florida

Established: 1980   Acreage: 172,845

Within a few miles of downtown Miami lies a quiet, almost pristine wilderness—a place of brilliant sunsets, warm, clear water, colorful reefs and tropical coral islands. Biscayne National Park, located only 21 miles east of Everglades National Park, allows the visitor to see South Florida the way the Indians and pirates saw it hundreds of years ago.

The park encompasses four important and interrelated biological systems: a mature mangrove forest growing on the fringe of the mainland; shallow Biscayne Bay, a nursery for fisheries; the underdeveloped, upper Florida Keys with their native vegetation; and the living coral reefs, found exclusively in the southeastern coastal region of the continental US.

In addition to the beautiful natural resources, Biscayne has an exciting history of Indians, Spanish explorers, pirates, sunken ships, buried treasure and rum-running. More recent historical activities include mahogany logging and pineapple and lime plantations. For most visitors, however, fishing, boating, snorkeling and diving are the popular activities.

Previous pages: Everglades in Florida is famous for its vast array of bird life, including the wood stork.

Far right, top: Blue herons nest seasonally in the protected refuge of Biscayne National Park.

Far right: The rare, shy manatee makes its home in the warm waters of Florida. This large animal, also called a sea cow, measures up to 15 feet (5 meters) in length. The survival of this harmless creature is threatened by motorboats and their propellers.

Right: The green sea turtle can be found in Biscayne—one of the few national parks that consists mostly of water.

CUTLER RIDGE

Coral Reef Drive (SW 152 Street)

Cutler Power Plant

CHICKEN KEY

PARK BOUNDARY

SAFETY VALVE

"1A"

SOLDIER KEY
(private)

FOWEY ROCKS

"2"

"3"

BREWSTER REEF

R "2"

"1B"

"4"

Numerous rocks

BLACK POINT PARK
(Dade County)

Coconut Palm Drive
(SW 248th Street)

Black Point

R "2"

"1"

Breakwater

Breakwater   Stakes and pipes mark channel

"3"

"5"

RAGGED KEYS
(private)

STAR REEF

Spoil Area

G "3"

ornamental lighthouse

harbor

Boca Chita Key

"7"

Fender Point

"4"

"2"

BOWLES BANK

R "6"

"5"

"4"   G "3"

"8"

R "8"

"X"

SANDS KEY

"9"

BISCAYNE BAY

"6"

SANDS CUT

University Dock

(private)

G "11 BS"

BACHE SHOAL

LEGARE ANCHORAGE

TRIUMPH REEF

W "2TR"

Park's eastern boundary extends to 60 ft (18m) depth

Convoy Point
Information Station
Park Headquarters

R "2"

Coon Point

Sea Grape Point

"13"

R "2"
G "1"

HOMESTEAD BAYFRONT PARK
(Dade County)

Elliott Key
Visitor Center

Point Adelle

"14"

"15"

Dome Reef

Homestead

R "2"
Elliott Key Harbor

"16"

LONG REEF

Pelican Bank

G "1"

Ott Point

MARGOT FISH SHOAL

Turkey Point Power Plant

"2"   platforms

Turkey Point

Little River

Billys Point

"17"

HAWK CHANNEL

Spoil Area

Petrel Point

"18"

Star Coral Reef

AJAX REEF

pile

Cooling Canals—Closed System

WEST ARSENICKER

Spoil Area

Schooner Wreck

Adams Key
Information Center

MANGROVE KEY

ARSENICKER KEY

R "8"

RUBICON KEYS

Dock

Christmas Point

"19"

GULF STREAM

Reid Key

CAESAR CREEK

R "20"

LONG ARSENICKER

G "9"

(private)

"4"

EAST ARSENICKER

"11"

CAESAR CREEK BANK

Mangrove Point

"12"

"13"

"3"

"2"

R "14"

"15"

TOTTEN KEY

PACIFIC REEF

"15A"

Spoil Area

OLD RHODES KEY

"21"

Elkhorn Coral Reef

(private)

SWAN KEY

GOLD KEY

BROAD CREEK

R "22"

R "14"

"12"

PALO ALTO KEY

"6"

ANGELFISH CREEK

"24"

"23"

CARD SOUND

"3"

R "2"

PUMPKIN KEY

Snapper Point

"2"

JOHN PENNEKAMP
CORAL REEF
STATE PARK
(protected area)

"16"

G "17"

KEY LARGO

"18"

G

"1"

KEY LARGO NATIONAL
MARINE SANCTUARY
(protected area)

"20"

"21"

R "2"

905

Whistle buoy
R "4"

North

0   1 Kilometer   3

0   1 Statute Mile

0   1 Nautical Mile

Everglades, Florida

Established: 1947 Acreage: 1,398,800

Long before the white man came the early Indians—the Colusas and the Tequestas—lived in the Evergaldes subsisting off the conches, oysters, clams, fish and game. The Indians that came later, the Miccosukees and Seminoles, arrived after the American Revolution. Creek Indians from states to the north, crowded out by white settlers came to Florida, and were gradually forced south to this region.

It was the Indians who gave the Everglades its perfect and poetic name—'Pa-Hay-Okee'—or grassy waters. The word 'everglades' actually means a marshy land covered with scattered tall grasses. A freshwater river six inches deep and 50 miles wide creeps seaward through the Everglades on a gradually-sloping riverbed. Along its long course, the water drops 15 feet, finally emptying into Florida Bay. The park was established to protect its unique biological features, and visitors need to take some time to walk the boardwalks and trails to understand and appreciate its mystique.

The Everglades is well known for its abundance and variety of birdlife. Roseate spoonbills, reddish egrets and rare great white herons live in Florida Bay. The park is also home to other rare and endangered species including the Florida panther, manatee, Everglades mink, green sea turtle, loggerhead turtle, peregrine falcon and crocodile. Other species, such as the Florida mangrove cuckoo, brown pelican and osprey, require special protection. Perhaps the Everglades is best known for the alligator, which has been dubbed 'Keeper of the Everglades.' The alligator cleans out the large holes in the Everglades' limestone bed that serve as a refuge during the dry winter season for fish, turtles, snails and other freshwater animals. In turn, these holes become the feeding grounds for alligators, birds and mammals until the rains come. Survivors—prey and predator—then leave the holes to repopulate the Everglades.

Despite the park's size, its environment is threatened by the disruptive activities of agriculture, industry and urban development around it. Life hangs precariously in the Everglades. Fresh water, although it seems to be everywhere, has been drastically blocked by man in South Florida. Conflicting demands compete for this precious water, leaving the Everglades struggling to survive. There are no other everglades in the world. Fortunately, the importance of the Everglades' ecosystem has been recognized by its designation as an International Biosphere Reserve and a World Heritage Site, but it will take human concern and prudent management to preserve the park's natural treasures.

Below: The alligator once risked extinction because its hide was prized for shoes and handbags, but thanks to protective measures, its numbers are now increasing.

Facing page: Among the many birds seen in the Everglades are the large and beautiful common egret.

Right: The unique grassy waters of the Everglades. No where else in the world is there a place quite like this.

Far right: The eastern diamondback rattlesnake inhabits the Everglades. Beware—these snakes are poisonous.

Right: *Park naturalists conduct guided tours of the Everglades, explaining the wonders of this strange and beautiful landscape.*

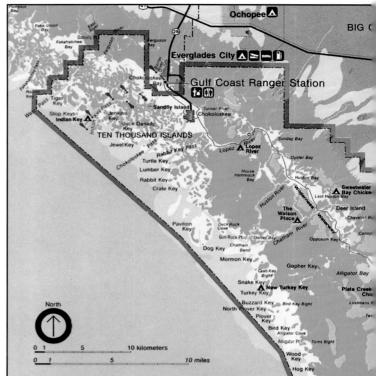

Below: *The American white pelican forages in the waters of Everglades National Park.*

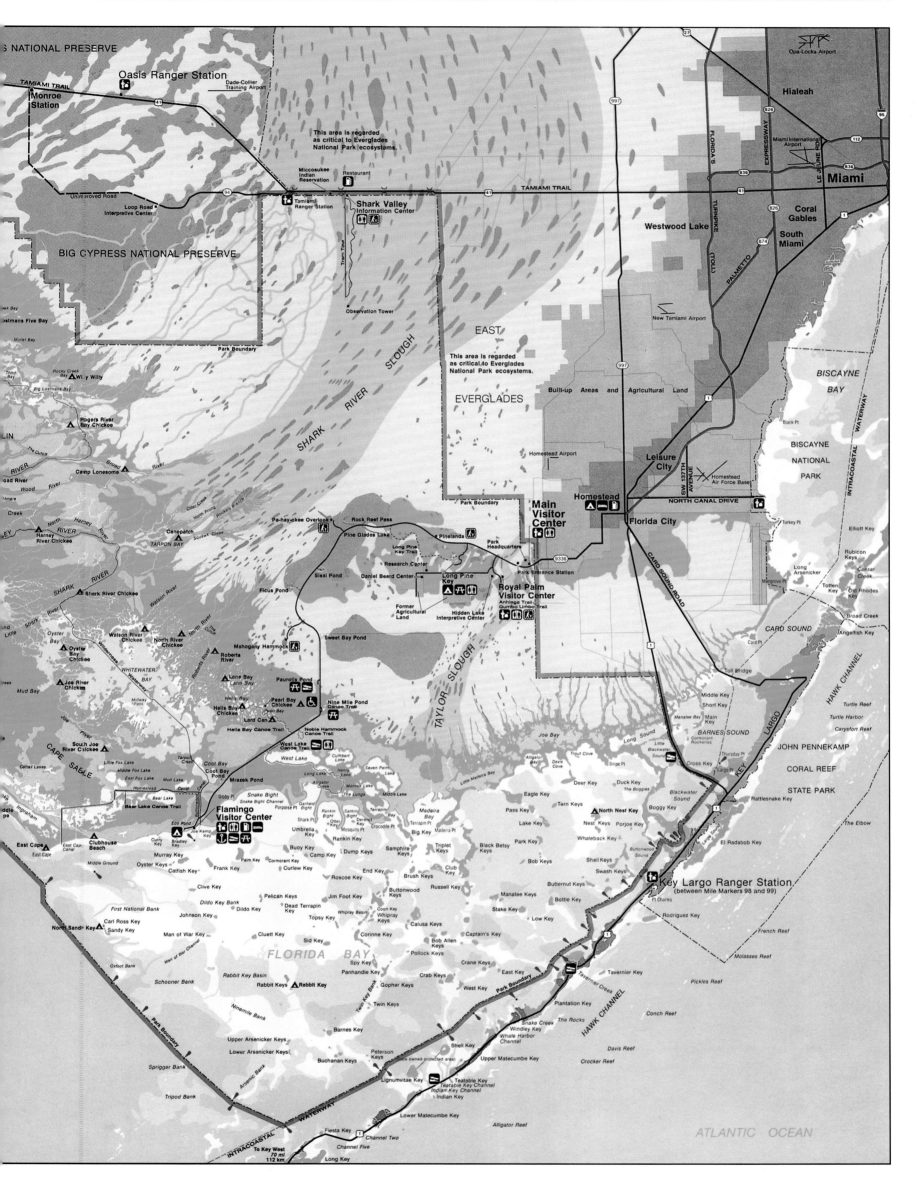

Great Smoky Mountains, North Carolina and Tennessee

Established: 1934   Acreage: 520,269

The Great Smoky Mountains, the majestic apex of the Appalachian Highlands, are a wildlands sanctuary preserving the world's finest examples of temperate deciduous forest. Over 100 species of trees—more than in all of Northern Europe—grow in the Great Smoky Mountains National Park. The name Smoky comes from the smoke-like haze enveloping the mountains, which stretch in sweeping troughs and mighty billows to the horizon.

The Smokies have a rich cultural history. For hundreds of years the Smokies were a part of the huge mountain empire of the Cherokee Indians under their great chief, Sequoyah. In the 1770s they sided with the British against the colonists. When white settlers came in from the north and from Virginia and South Carolina, the Indians began to be crowded out. During the winter of 1838, the government marched most of them to a new home in Oklahoma. In the years that followed, the land was worked by hardy and determined Scotch-Irish settlers who developed a unique way of life in their isolated surroundings.

When the park was established over 1200 tracts of the land purchased were farms owned by these people. As a result of this purchase, the park has an unequalled collection of log buildings, including large, two-story dwellings and grist mills, totalling over 77 historic structures in all. Restored log cabins and barns punctuate the park's wild qualities, making for a delightful mix of forest wildlands and an outdoor museum of pioneer life.

From the Tennessee side, at Cades Cove, there is an 11-mile loop drive through a pastoral Smokies scene with restored buildings and an old mill. The Oconaluftee Visitor Center is the first stop on the North Carolina side. The nearby Pioneer Farmstead lets visitors see how the early mountain people lived. Just up the road into the park is Mingus Mill, a large water-powered mill for grinding corn. Sugarlands and Oconaluftee are connected by the Newfound Gap Road, which the Appalachian Trail crosses. The roads are only an introduction to the Smokies, however. Some 900 miles of trails thread the whole of the Smokies' natural fabric—its waterfalls, coves and rushing streams.

Below: Great Smoky Mountains National Park has more than its share of black bear. Though they may look harmless, they are wild animals and can be dangerous.

Above: *Enveloped in its namesake haze, the Great Smoky Mountains seem to roll endlessly into the horizon.*

Left: *The many trails of the park invite hikers to explore the majestic beauty of the wild Appalachian highlands. Trails cover every degree of difficulty, from paved walkways to steep mountain paths.*

Right: *From high atop this vista point, park visitors have a view of the incredible forests of the Smokies.*

Far right: *When the sun sets, the mountains take on a golden hue. It is no wonder that this park draws more visitors than any other national park in the United States.*

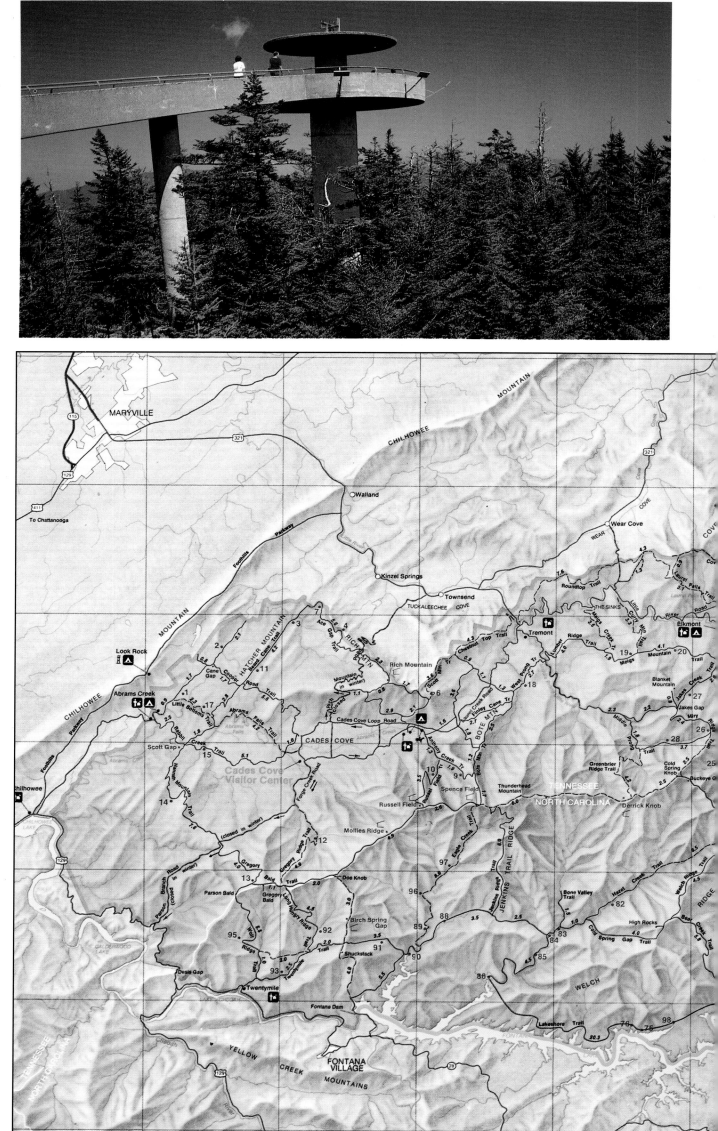

Hot Springs, Arkansas

Established: 1921   Acreage: 5824

Hot Springs, 'the Valley of the Vapors,' was a revered and sacred place to the Indians, who believed it was the home of the Great Spirit. This was neutral ground. Here a warrior, regardless of his tribe or tongue, could lay aside his arms and bathe in peace. It is believed that the hot springs were used by explorer Hernando de Soto during his travels in 1540. By the

early 1800s, bathers came to Hot Springs seeking cures for their ailments. Popular sentiment called for reserving the land for public use, and in 1832 the federal government took the unprecedented step of setting aside four sections of land as a reservation—the first in the nation's history. In the early years of the twentieth century monumental bathhouses were built to cater to the crowds of health seekers.

According to *Cutter's Official Guide to Hot Springs, Arkansas*, first published in 1873, the 'topography of Hot Springs is very similar to that of Carlsbad, Germany, while the pine-clad foothills of the Ozarks afford both healthful exercise and inspiring scenery.' Further, there are '46 hot springs with an average temperature of 135 degrees Fahrenheit, the hottest being 157 degrees. They discharge about 800,000 gallons per day.'

The most important thing about Hot Springs' thermal water is that it is naturally sterile. Analysis of the waters has proved that chemical and radioactive properties are similar for all the springs. Today, the bathhouses are owned and operated by private concessioners and are all guaranteed an adequate supply of water from the same source. The distribution system operates from two large underground reservoirs on Hot Springs Mountain, both of which feed by gravity to the bathhouses, where operators blend the waters to regulate the bath temperature. A full range of options is available: tub and pool baths, shower, steam cabinet, hot and cold packs, whirlpool and massage or alcohol rub. Visitors to the park can also hike amid the flowering trees of the Zig Zag Mountains.

Right: As long as 10,000 years ago, people came to the hot springs to relax. Then all the springs looked something like this one; today, however, all but two springs are covered to prevent contamination of the water. The two uncovered springs are for display.

Below: Hot Springs is nestled in the Zig Zag Mountains, which are covered with dense forests of oak, hickory and short-leaf pines.

Above: Hot water cascades down the mountain in a spectacular display of water, rock and algae.

Right: Visitors to the park can hike the many trails through the mountains and relax amid the lush vegetation. With its warm and pleasant climate year-round, Hot Springs is truly a paradise.

Mammoth Cave, Kentucky

Established: 1941   Acreage: 52,370

From the beginning, underground explorers doubted that they would ever find the end of Mammoth Cave. The cave system goes on and on for more than 300 miles of known passages, and there is yet more cave to be explored. It is the longest cave in the world, with none others even coming close. In this huge subterranean world, there are giant vertical shafts, from the towering 192-foot-high Mammoth Dome to the 105-foot-deep Bottomless Pit. Some passages and rooms are decorated with sparkling white gypsum crystals, while others are filled with the colorful shapes of stalactites, stalagmites and other formations. The area is known as a karst landscape, a region of limestone caves, underground rivers, springs and sinkholes.

Water has been the guiding force in the creation of this landscape. Underground water working in cracks and between rock layers has carved out Mammoth Cave's long, horizontal passageways over the past few million years. Mammoth's huge vertical shafts, called pits and domes, have been created by groundwater seeping downward through sinkholes or cracks behind the edge of the protective hard layer of sandstone that overlies much of the cave.

Although the cave was explored by prehistoric Indians as many as 4000 years ago, modern-day encounters with the cave supposedly began in the late 1790s, when a hunter chasing a bear fell into its gaping entrance. The cave became commercially valuable during the War of 1812 between the United States and Britain. Cave sediments with abundant quantities of nitrate, an essential ingredient of gunpowder, were mined by slaves during the war. By the war's end, Mammoth was famous and soon became one of the nation's popular attractions. During the 1800s and early 1900s the cave was host to all kinds of events—weddings, stage performances. Even a tuberculosis hospital was established.

Today, Mammoth Cave National Park provides the extraordinary world of the underground and the more familiar surface world of oak and hickory forests, meandering rivers and woodland wildlife.

Above right: Mammoth Cave National Park offers the opportunity to explore a fascinating subterranean world.

Right: The forces of water—and time—carved the stalactites, stalagmites and columns of limestone.

Facing page: The sheer size of Mammoth Cave is overwhelming—passages stretch on for miles, domes reach vast heights and pits seem to go to the very center of the earth.

Shenandoah, Virginia

Established: 1935   Acreage: 195,057

Shenandoah National Park lies astride a section of the Blue Ridge, which forms the eastern bulwark of the Appalachian Mountains between Pennsylvania and Georgia. Providing vistas of the spectacular landscape is the 105-mile-long Skyline Drive, a winding road that runs along the Blue Ridge through the length of the park. The park contains 60 mountain peaks ranging from 2000 to 4000 feet in elevation. When it was established in 1935, it became only the second national park east of the Mississippi River.

The story of the park includes 9000 years of continuous human involvement with the land. Indians lived here long before the Europeans discovered it, living off the land, picking what they could use from the native plants and hunting wild game. By 1800, white settlement of the lowlands around the park was generally complete. While the valleys were being colonized, the mountains themselves remained uninhabited. As long as land was readily available in the valleys, farmers had no need to move to the less hospitable mountain slopes. Later, good land was hard to find, and people moved farther up the mountains.

It was these subsistence farmers who, in the mid-1800s, established the celebrated 'mountain culture' of this area of the Appalachians. As the people moved into the mountain hollows in increasing numbers, they began to adversely affect the land. Game, once plentiful, disappeared. Soil erosion increased as land was cleared for use. By 1900 the land was wearing out and people began to move off the ridge. In 1936, President Franklin D Roosevelt initiated a novel experiment in returning an overused area to its original beauty. Croplands and pastures soon became overgrown with shrubs, locusts, and pine. In turn, oak, hickory and other trees that make up a mature deciduous forest were growing within the boundaries of the park. The vegetative regeneration has been so complete that in 1976 Congress designated two-fifths of the park as a wilderness. The area now teems with wildflowers, strawberries and blueberries, as well as many species of wildlife—deer, bobcat, bear, turkey and smaller animals, such as chipmunk, raccoon, skunk, opossum and gray squirrel. Over 200 species of birds have been recorded. The park is also home to several species of salamanders and snakes.

Although the park's primary purpose is to preserve the natural resources, traces of the human story remain to be explored. The remains of the mountain people's homes, barns, hog pens and fruit cellars exist throughout the park as piles of logs, a few standing walls and lone chimneys. A few significant historic buildings, such as President Hoover's Camp, have been preserved.

Far right, top: The heart of Shenandoah's beauty is its forests—over 95 percent of the park is covered with lush forests with 100 species of trees.

Far right, middle: The barred owl is a permanent resident of the park, but many species of birds find their way here on their southward migration.

Far right, bottom: Deer are frequently seen from the trails that crisscross the ridges and valleys, and the hills and hollows of this enchanted land.

Facing page: Scenic Skyline Drive provides panoramic vistas of the spectacular Shenandoah Valley.

Below: A family enjoys a peaceful moment of solitude as the sun sets on the Blue Ridge Mountains, painting the horizon pink and purple.

Virgin Islands, American Virgin Islands

Established: 1956   Acreage: 14,695

When Christopher Columbus charted a chain of green, mountainous islands in 1493, the resulting Spanish claims began two hundred years of international wars for supremacy of the West Indies. In 1717, Denmark took control, starting a period during which slave labor built many sugar and cotton plantations. Two centuries later the United States bought the Virgin Islands from Denmark.

St John, the smallest and least populated of the three main American Virgin Islands, is famous for white coral sand beaches, turquoise water, scenic mountain roads, trails and quiet coves. Over one-half of the land and most of the shoreline waters of this beautiful island have been set aside as Virgin Islands National Park. Visitors can hike on trails crossing the rugged natural beauty of the island or can snorkel the mysterious undersea world. Swimming, scuba diving, underwater photography, fishing and sailing are other popular activities. Brush-covered ruins of the eighteenth and nineteenth century sugar plantations and petroglyphs carved in stone entice visitors to explore its human history.

Trunk Bay has one of the best beaches in the world and offers an underwater nature trail for snorkelers. The Leinster Bay area contains a mangrove swamp, reef flat and the partially restored ruins of the Annaberg sugar mill factory complex. Located on St John's rugged north shore, it is reminiscent of an ancient European castle, constructed of fitted stone, native coral and yellow and red Danish ballast brick. The Danes, Dutch and slaves toiled here to produce crude brown sugar, rich dark molasses and strong rum for export to North America and Europe. Coral Bay, the site of the first sugar plantation, was settled in 1717 and was chosen for its well-protected harbor.

On the South Shore, Salt Pond Bay and Lameshur Bay remain calm during the winter ground seas that make snorkeling and swimming hazardous on the North Shore beaches. The drive to Lameshur Bay, which requires a four-wheel drive vehicle, crosses a rugged and historic area that was once known for bay oil, lime juice and cattle production. In Reef Bay Valley, visitors to the park discover petroglyphs (rock carvings) by West African natives and Taino Indians. The valley also contains the ruins of the Reef Bay Estate House and steampowered sugar mills, the last to operate on the island.

There are no native animals living on the Virgin Islands, and only two varieties of snakes, both harmless. Of the 100 to 150 different species of birds here, many are migrants, often flying back and forth from the US mainland, rather than from other tropical places. The mongoose, brought here from India, is a pest, killing chickens and birds. There are no highways on the Islands—the sea is their highway.

Below: The sparkling blue waters of Leinster Bay beckon swimmers, snorkelers, scuba divers and sailors.

Right: The ruins of the Annaberg Plantation—once a vast sugar mill factory complex.

Below: Trunk Bay, famous for its white sand beaches, is a paradise for sunbathers and snorkelers alike.

THE
PLAINS

Badlands, South Dakota

Established: 1978   Acreage: 243,302

French-Canadian trappers were among early European visitors to the Badlands, calling the region 'bad lands to travel across.' Badlands National Park is a remnant of one of the world's great grasslands, stretching from southern Alberta and Saskatchewan almost to Mexico, and from the Rockies to Indiana. Rain, wind and frost have carved steep canyons, sharp ridges, gullies, spires and knobs from the rolling Dakota prairie, providing a look into the pace of geologic change.

The oldest formation in the Badlands is a 65-million-year-old layer of black shale that formed on the bottom of an ancient sea. About 37 million years ago, the Badlands area was a broad, marshy plain crossed by sluggish streams. The animals thrived on the jungle and marsh plants that grew here. Toward the end of the Oligocene Epoch, volcanoes spewed huge volumes of ash into the atmosphere, which eventually became the whitish layer near the top of the Badlands formations. Slowly, the climate changed and became drier. The animals also changed, with grass eaters emerging.

The Arikara are the first known Indians to have lived in the area, but by the mid-eighteenth century the Sioux Indians dominated. Their culture, based on hunting the large bison herds that roamed the plains, flourished for the next one hundred years. Then the migration of Eastern settlers, miners and, finally, the US Army sealed the fate of the Sioux at the infamous battle at Wounded Knee in the winter of 1890. The arrival of the white man also led to a similar fate for some of the large plains animals—the gray wolf, the elk and the grizzly. Although almost wiped out, bison and bighorn sheep have been reintroduced to the prairie.

Other wildlife—pronghorn antelope, prairie dogs, cottontail rabbits, mule deer and meadowlarks—inhabit the Badlands. Among the Badland's wildflowers, Barr's milkvetch and Visher's buckwheat show contrasting adaptations to the dry climate. The milkvetch, a perennial that can live for as long as 50 years, has a long root that anchors the plant and reaches down deep into the soil for water. In contrast, the buckwheat blooms each spring when the rains of April and May bring to life the seeds that have lain buried during the long winter.

Previous pages: The delicate beauty of a rainbow provides a striking contrast to the awesome cliffs of Badlands National Park.

*Below: To the early French settlers, the tall spires of the Badlands were **les mauvaises terres à traverser**—bad lands to travel across—but to us today they are a scenic and geologic wonder.*

Left: Hiking the steep ridges of Badlands is only for the stout of heart.

Right: The sharp ridges and spires are punctuated with grassy tables—grazing areas for bighorn sheep.

Below: Though their numbers are now greatly reduced, bison have been restored to the high plains of the Badlands, where they once roamed by the thousands.

These pages: The white man's arrival in the Badlands nearly wiped out the sure-footed bighorn sheep. Fortunately, bighorns have been successfully re-introduced to their rightful place among the cliffs.

Elk Island, Alberta

Established: 1913   Acreage: 48,000

The park is located in the Beaver Hills, a landscape of water-filled hollows and rolling hills rising above the surrounding plains. The hills are large mounds of rock, dirt and gravel left behind by the retreating glaciers 10,000 years ago; aspen forests and spruce bogs now characterize this elevated 'island' in the prairie. Surrounding Elk Island lies the landscape of man—grainfields, pastures and towns. But within the fenced boundaries, a trace of what was once natural to the Beaver Hills still survives—forests and meadowlands, quiet lakes and beaver ponds. The park has over 250 lakes and ponds, the largest of which are Astotin and Tawawik.

For centuries, the Sarcee Indians lived in the area, making little change in the harmony of life that existed in the hills. Eventually the Sarcee were forced onto the surrounding plains by the Cree, who supplied white fur traders with the pelts of beaver—already trapped to near extinction in the east. When the Cree moved in the late 1800s, the land seemed empty. Fires had scarred the land—no longer were there large tracts of spruce, tamarack and poplar to shelter the few remaining herds of elk—another animal that was close to extinction.

The concern of local residents was aroused. The first step toward conservation in the Beaver Hills was the creation of a federal timber reserve in 1899. Soon after, local conservationists called for an elk sanctuary to preserve an overhunted herd. Today Elk Island is also a haven for the once nearly extinct bison. For 400,000 years, millions of plains bison roamed the grasslands of North America, but within the span of a hundred years this huge animal was brought to the brink of extinction when European settlers hunted them for food and hides.

In 1907, the Canadian government, seeking to rescue the bison from extinction, purchased the largest remaining herd and shipped them to Elk Island until a fence could be completed at Buffalo National Park. When the herd was moved to its final destination, about 50 bison evaded the round up and remained at Elk Island. From this small group grew today's herd. The park is also home to a herd of wood bison, which is kept isolated from the plains bison to ensure that the two subspecies remain pure.

In addition to restoring the bison, Elk Island is involved in the conservation of all wildlife, including moose, deer, beaver and coyote. Other mammals found in the park include shrews, chipmunks and mink. The lakes and marshes of the park are home to many of the 230 species of birds seen at Elk Island, including ducks, gulls, terns, grebes and loons. Land birds can be spotted in the branches of poplar, spruce and birch trees. Within the park's boundaries, rare species of marsh marigold and several types of lilies are found. Though small in size, Elk Island National Park has played a large role in conserving Canada's animal and plant life.

Right: White-tailed deer move freely in and out of Elk Island, jumping or squeezing under the seven-foot boundary fence.

Below: Park visitors stroll along the 'Living Waters Boardwalk' floating interpretive trail.

Left: Astotin Lake is the largest and deepest (21 feet) in Elk Island, and has 17 islands.

Below: Largely because of the conservation efforts of Elk Island, the plains bison is no longer considered an endangered species. More than 100,000 plains bison are now found in parks, zoos and private ranches across North America. The park is also home to a herd of wood bison. Wood bison are taller and larger, have a taller and squarer hump, are darker in color, and have a smaller, more pointed beard than plains bison.

Grasslands, Saskatchewan

Established: 1988   Acreage: 224,071

In September 1988, the Government of Canada and the Government of Saskatchewan signed an agreement establishing Grasslands National Park, an area on the Canadian-US border that contains one of the last remnants of native, mixed grass prairie in North America. The mixed prairie vegetation supports a wide variety of wildlife, including pronghorn antelope, ferruginous hawks, prairie rattlesnake and sage grouse. Black-tailed prairie dogs build their colonies along the Frenchman River Valley, the only place where this little creature can be seen in its natural habitat. The rare and endangered prairie falcon can also be seen in Grasslands.

The weathered landforms of the Killdeer Badlands dot the rolling plains. Here Sir George Mercier Dawson, geologist and naturalist to Her Majesty's North American Boundary Commission, discovered dinosaur remains in 1874. Grasslands also contains 'Sinking Hill,' a fault-like formation 66 yards wide and 11 yards deep, which is sinking roughly six and a half feet a year.

Tepee rings, projectile points and other artifacts reveal a colorful human history. Plains Indians once roamed here in search of bison, and the area was a favorite hunting ground for the nomadic Métis during the early days of the Red River Settlement. After the battle of the Little Bighorn, Sitting Bull and his Sioux followers took refuge in the Grasslands area. A few homesteaders briefly settled in the region, but moved on when they found the land ill-suited for farming. In their wake came ranchers, who established a flourishing industry that continues to this day.

Because the park is in the early stages of development, visitor facilities are not yet available, and the roads there are primarily for access by local ranchers. Thus visitors to the park will find a wilderness, much as it was when the bison and Indians roamed the plains.

Above right, top: *Grasslands is populated with numerous black-tailed prairie dogs. These social creatures live in colonies along the Frenchman River Valley.*

Above right, middle: *The burrowing owl makes its home in the prairies of Grasslands National Park.*

Right: *The gently rolling hills of Grasslands are one of the few remaining areas of mixed grass prairie in North America.*

Facing page, top: *The sage grouse is almost always found wherever there is sagebrush.*

Facing page, bottom: *Pronghorns are the fastest land animals in North America. In short bursts of speed, they can reach up to 60 miles per hour.*

Prince Albert, Saskatchewan

Established: 1927 Acreage: 957,440

Prince Albert National Park lies in central Saskatchewan, where prairie gradually gives way to the lake country of the north. The park's unique quality is determined mostly by its position halfway between Canada's south and north. The park's gently rolling terrain is a mosaic of spruce bogs, large, cold lakes and aspen uplands.

Wildlife populations reflect the changing vegetation. Moose, wolves, caribou and loons capture the essence of the northern forests. Elk, deer and badger inhabit the aspen parkland. Black bear, beaver, red fox and a small herd of free-roaming bison also make their home in the park. This diversity of animals makes wildlife watching a favorite visitor pastime, and a drive along one of the park roads or a hike through the woods at dawn or dusk may provide a glimpse of one of the park's inhabitants.

The park also contains a breeding colony of white pelicans on Lavalee Lake (historically known as Pelican Lake). The fourth largest pelican breeding colony in Canada, it is the only colony protected within a national park. Pelicans require an undisturbed area for breeding, and in recent years a number of their colonies have been destroyed by human disturbance. Access to the lake is strictly controlled during the spring and summer months to ensure that this impressive species continues.

In addition to the pelican, the park protects some of the last remaining fescue grasslands found in North America. Outside of national parks, very little fescue grasslands remain in their unaltered state. Roughly 90 percent of these grasslands have been altered by ploughing, mowing or haying.

World acclaimed naturalist Grey Owl lived at Beaver Lodge on Ajawaan Lake. It was here that he raised Jellyroll and Rawhide, the beaver pair Grey Owl immortalized in his writings. Grey Owl was born Archibald Belaney in Hastings in Sussex County, England. In 1905, as a child, he moved to Canada and lived the life of an Indian in the Temagami and Biscotasing areas of Ontario. Following the publication of his

articles, Grey Owl was employed by the National Parks Service of Canada to promote public interest in conservation. After his death in 1938, his pet beavers were returned to the wild, and later reports revealed an increase in the beaver population in the Ajawaan Lake area.

In 1690 the fur trade in Saskatchewan began. Although the park area played a role as a prime hunting ground, it was bypassed by the early explorers because the main waterways, the Churchill and Saskatchewan Rivers, passed north and south of the region. Not until other areas had been exploited did trappers and traders move into the vicinity.

Previous pages: Sparkling stands of aspen are found throughout Prince Albert National Park.

Far right: Cast your line into cool northern waters for lake trout, northern pike and walleye.

Below: Prince Albert is a sanctuary for the striking white pelican. In recent years, a number of colonies throughout their range have been destroyed by man's presence.

Riding Mountain, Manitoba

Established: 1929   Acreage: 735,360

Rising dramatically out of a sea of farmland is an island of wilderness—Riding Mountain National Park. Situated on a ridge called the Manitoba Escarpment, the park sits 1430 feet (436 meters) above the prairie. The view from the top of this shale ridge stretches 50 miles (80 km) to the east. This highland plateau, lying at the center of the North American continent, is a place where the plant and animal communities of the north, east and west meet, creating a mosaic of diverse plant and animal life.

The lower slopes of the escarpment are graced by stands of eastern deciduous forest. Here are the elm, ash and oak more commonly seen along the shore of the Great Lakes. High areas of the park are covered with evergreen forest—white and black spruce, jack pine, balsam fir and tamarack. To the

west, at the escarpment's edge, white poplar opens into meadows of rough fescue prairie. In the summer the grasses mingle with a pageantry of wildflowers.

The animal population is as diverse as the landscape. Bald eagles and osprey, as well as beavers, make their home near the wild streams and lakes. Elk gather in sedge meadows to graze while, nearby, wolf packs wait their turn to strike. In the woodlands, the silent lynx stalks its prey. Other mammals include black bear, coyote and cougar. A small herd of bison inhabit a fenced range near Lake Audy.

The park is famous for the size and number of its fish. Northern pike is the main game fish, and specimens up to 29 pounds (13 kilograms) have been taken from Clear Lake. Lake, rainbow and brook trout, walleye and whitefish are the other species that populate the lakes of Riding Mountain.

The fascinating, varied landscape and wildlife can be explored through the network of hiking and riding trails. Fishing, camping, swimming, canoeing and boating are other popular pastimes. Winter recreational activities include ice fishing, cross country and downhill skiing, and snowshoeing.

Right: Crossing the escarpment on horseback is a fun way to explore the diverse landscape of the park.

Below: Elk can frequently be spotted in Riding Mountain National Park.

Right: The Interpretive Center oversees a number of programs—from on-site exhibits to naturalist-led activities—to inform visitors of the park's natural and human history.

Far right: The view from the top of the escarpment extends as far as the eye can see.

Below: A spectacular sunset on Clear Lake. The lakes in Riding Mountain are home to herons, osprey and eagles.

Theodore Roosevelt, North Dakota

Established: 1978   Acreage: 70,416

In the North Dakota Badlands, where many of Theodore Roosevelt's personal concerns gave rise to his later environmental efforts, he is remembered with a national park that bears his name. Roosevelt first came to Dakota to hunt, but found that the bison had virtually been exterminated. The ranges upon which countless numbers of bison had once roamed were covered with native grasses that were well-suited for the grazing of cattle. Roosevelt soon became interested in the cattle business and joined two other men as partners in the Maltese Cross Ranch. The next year he returned and established a second open-range ranch, the Elkhorn, as his own operation.

The park consists of two separate areas, known as the North and South units, and the Elkhorn Ranch site. In the park's North Unit visitors may encounter longhorns, similar to the cattle raised by ranchers in Roosevelt's time. The park is also home to herds of bison that graze the Badlands as they once did, though now their numbers are few. The efforts of Roosevelt and other conservationists helped to save the bison

from extinction. Mule deer, whitetail deer and prairie dogs also inhabit the park. More than 125 species of birds, many of which are songbirds, can be found (and heard) within the park. Near the visitor center is a series of slump blocks, huge sections of bluff that gradually slide intact to the valley floor. This is not uncommon in the Badlands, where canyon walls are too steep to support a top-heavy formation.

At the museum in the South Unit one can see personal items of Theodore Roosevelt's, ranching artifacts and natural history displays. The restored Maltese Cross cabin is nearby. A major feature of the South Unit is a paved, 36-mile, scenic loop which lets visitors explore the landscape. Although the park may seem barren and inhospitable, the land is rich in geologic history. Many areas of the park contain bands of lignite coal and petrified trees, both of which were formed from the trees that lay buried under sediment on the alluvial plain during the Tertiary period. The lignite coal continues to shape the Badlands. Lightning can ignite the coal, which then burns for many years, heating the rocks above. The heated rocks grow harder and are then more resistant to erosion.

On the edge of the South Unit is the DeMores State Historic Site, a 27-room chateau that the Marquis DeMores built in 1884. The marquis, an acquaintance of Theodore Roosevelt, was a wealthy French nobleman who built a slaughterhouse to process beef from the large local herds for shipping to market in the then new refrigerated railroad cars.

Below: Late summer on the prairie in Theodore Roosevelt National Park, with the bluffs rising in the distance.

Above: A lone bison climbs the buttes of the Badlands. Through the efforts of Theodore Roosevelt and others, bison were saved from extinction. Today bison graze the Badlands as they once did, but now they are confined to the park.

Above right: Although barren, this harsh and rocky landscape is nonetheless striking.

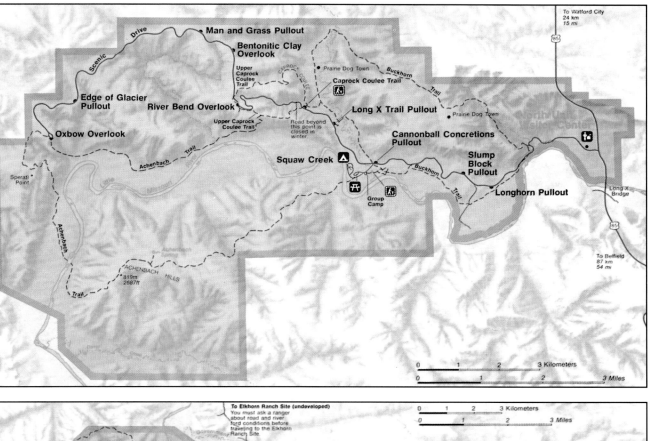

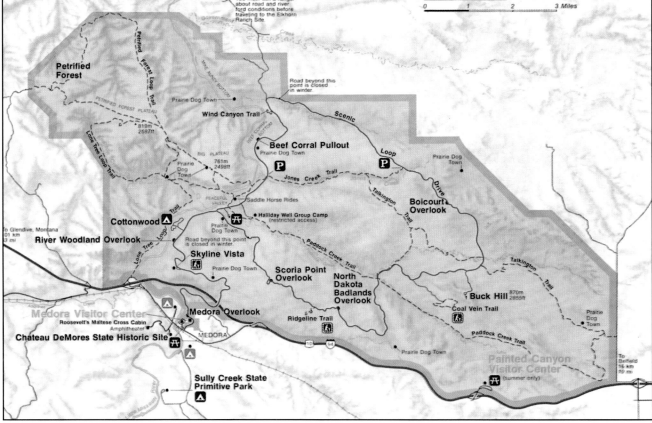

Wind Cave, South Dakota

Established: 1903   Acreage: 28,292

Wind Cave, like Carlsbad Caverns was formed by the action of water. It lies on a layer of limestone rock 300 to 600 feet thick. Beginning about 60 million years ago the rain fell into the cracks in this limestone layer and gradually dissolved it away from the harder rock. The temperature in the cave never changes—it remains at 47 degrees Fahrenheit.

An early handbill proclaimed the cave 'the Great Freak of Nature.' Although native Americans may have known of the cave, it was not discovered by white men until 1881, when Jesse and Tom Bingham heard a loud whistling noise. The sound led them to a small hole in the ground, the cave's only natural opening. A wind was said to be blowing with such force that it knocked off Jesse's hat. That wind, which gave the cave its name, is created by differences between atmospheric pressures in the cave and outside.

This underground world is a complex maze of more than 40 miles of mapped passageways, containing boxwork, popcorn and frostwork formations, and over 1000 passages are yet to be explored. Early adventurers found chocolate-colored crystals, formations resembling faces of animals and chambers that inspired names such as 'The Garden of Eden' and 'The Dungeon.' Reports of these strange discoveries drew tourists to the area. Before the cave was protected by the National Park Service, enterprising local residents blasted open passages, guided tourists through for a fee and sold cave specimens.

In addition to the wonders of the cave, the park serves as a wildlife sanctuary, established as such in 1912. The park's primary objective as a sanctuary was the restoration of populations of bison, elk and pronghorn to the Black Hills. By the

late 1800s these animals had been decimated, mostly because of uncontrolled hunting. Perhaps no other animal symbolizes the West as dramatically as the American bison. In 1800, an estimated 40 million bison roamed the plains, yet by 1883, there were no wild bison in the United States. By 1900, there were less than 600 left in North America. The majority of the 40 million animals were killed in a 55-year period, beginning in 1830. Starting with 14 bison donated by the Bronx Zoo in 1913, the herd today numbers about 350.

Mule deer, prairie dogs, cottontail rabbits, coyotes, badgers, rattlesnakes and numerous kinds of birds also live in the prairies and forests of Wind Hill. Located near the middle of the country, the park is home to plant and animal species found in both the East and the West. It is not unusual to find pinyon jays and ponderosa pines from the West and bluebirds and American elms from the East.

Wind Cave is really two parks— the cave and the prairie above. The prairie is home to a wide variety of wildlife, including pronghorn antelope (far right). These swift mammals are truly American natives, found nowhere else in the world. Pronghorns have roamed the plains of North America for at least the last million years.

Also found on the prairie is a small herd of bison (below), a reminder of the vast herds that once covered the plains of North America.

Above and overleaf: The park offers a number of tours through the dark and mysterious passages of Wind Cave. Tours range from a candlelight tour that recreates the explorations of the past to a spelunking tour that explores the unlit, unpaved areas of the cave.

Left: The lure of the unknown has drawn visitors to Wind Cave since its discovery over 100 years ago.

Wood Buffalo, Alberta and Northwest Territories

Established: 1922   Acreage: 11,072,000

Spread out on the northern plains of western Canada, straddling the border between the province of Alberta and the Northwest Territories, Wood Buffalo National Park offers a landscape where enormous rivers meander through a subarctic wilderness of bogs, forests, lakes and meadows. The park is one of the world's largest, covering an area larger than Switzerland. Situated on the northern boreal plains, the plants here are typical of the boreal forest zone found in North America and northern Europe and Asia. Lush forests of white and black spruce, jack pine, tamarack, black poplar and trembling aspen fill this vast, magnificent wilderness.

Right: Water-filled sinkholes—a feature of a karst landscape. Surface and ground water dissolve the soft bedrock, creating underground rivers, caves and sinkholes.

Below: The namesake of Wood Buffalo National Park—the bison is the largest terrestrial animal in North America.

Here, animals such as moose, wolves, lynx, black bear, eagles and ravens thrive. Smaller mammals, such as shrews, bats, woodchucks, chipmunks, snowshoe hare and squirrels, are also found in the forests and meadows of the park. Wood Buffalo National Park, as the name implies, is home to a herd of 3000 to 4000 bison, the largest free-roaming herd in the world. From 1925 to 1927, roughly 7000 bison were transported from Buffalo Park to the newly established Wood Buffalo National Park. An unforeseen consequence of the transplant was the interbreeding between the transplanted plains bison and the resident wood buffalo. By 1934, the herd had grown to 12,000, but the bison were hybrids and it was feared that the wood bison as a subspecies was lost. Today the herd has stabilized at 3000 to 4000 hybrid bison. A small herd of wood bison was discovered and has been transferred to other protected areas in Canada to ensure that the subspecies survives.

This spacious and wild park also contains the last nesting grounds of the rare and endangered whooping crane. Hundreds and thousands of geese, ducks and other waterfowl inhabit the Peace-Athabasca Delta. Out of the 227 species of birds that have been observed in the park, 142 nest here during the summer, but only 25 species are able to endure the harsh winters. The delta also supports large populations of muskrat and beaver and is the spawning ground for goldeye and walleye.

Recent studies indicate that Wood Buffalo contains the most extensive gypsum karst terrain in the world: a remarkable landscape of sinkholes, underground rivers, caves and sunken valleys. The park's Salt Plains are unique in Canada, with their white, salt-encrusted mud flats, unusual salt-tolerant plants and saline meadows dotted with islands of spruce trees and shrubs.

Most of the park remains in its original wilderness state, but areas are set aside for camping, picnicking, boating and swimming.

Above: *The Salt Plains. Salty water emerges from springs at the base of a low escarpment and flows across flat, open areas. Only the few species of plant life capable of tolerating high levels of salt can grow here.*

Right: *The whooping crane is the most famous of the park's many species of birds. These great white birds come from the Aransas Refuge in Texas to nest each spring and then leave in early October.*

These pages: Wood Buffalo National Park was established to protect the last remaining herd of wood bison—the larger, darker northern relatives of the plains bison. Later, plains bison were brought to the park, and the two species interbred. As a result, most—if not all—of the bison in the park are hybrids. A small herd of pure wood bison is protected in Elk Island National Park in Alberta.

THE ROCKIES

Arches, Utah

Established: 1971   Acreage: 73,379

Arches National Park, which has the greatest density of natural arches in the world, lies atop an underground salt bed. Wind and water, extreme temperatures and underground salt movement created the red rock pinnacles, spires, balanced rocks, sandstone fins and arches that make the area a sightseer's mecca. Early explorers thought the huge arches were, like Stonehenge in England, the remnants of a long lost culture.

The more than 200 catalogued arches range in size from a three-foot opening (the minimum considered an arch) to Landscape Arch (105-foot), a ribbon of rock that measures 291 feet from base to base. All stages of arch formation and decay are found here. Delicate Arch, all that remains of a bygone fin, stands on the edge of a canyon, with the white-capped LaSal Mountains for a backdrop.

Covering the salt bed was millions of years worth of debris, which had been compressed into rock. Salt is an unstable substance and the salt bed below Arches was no match for the weight of this thick cover of rock. Under the pressure of the rock layers it shifted, buckled, liquified and repositioned itself, thrusting the earth layers upward into domes. Entire sections dropped into cavities; others turned on edge. When overlaying areas of earth sank into cavities, great fractures, called 'faults,' formed. A 2500-foot displacement of earth is obvious in the Moab Fault, which can be seen from the visitor center.

Green pinyon pines and juniper trees provide a contrast to the red sandstone terrain. In spring, when conditions are right, pockets of the park brim with wildflowers. Wildlife here is typical of the sparse pinyon and juniper forests of the Great Basin Desert. Although most species are nocturnal, visitors occasionally glimpse mule deer, kit fox, jackrabbits and cottontails, kangaroo rats and small reptiles. Blue pinyon jays, golden eagles and redtailed hawks reside in the park, and bald eagles and peregrine falcons have been sighted.

The park also contains the site of Wolfe Ranch, a small cattle operation once run by John Wesley Wolfe, a disabled Civil War veteran, and his son Fred. An aged log cabin, root cellar and corral provide a look at life 100 years ago.

Above right: South Window (left) and North Window (right). The people standing in North Window give a sense of the overwhelming size of these formations.

Delicate Arch (right) and Balanced Rock (far right), two of the well known landmarks in Arches National Park.

Facing Page: Pine Tree Arch, so named for the pine tree in the center of the arch.

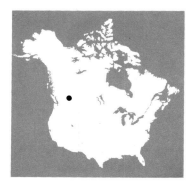

Banff, Alberta

Established: 1887   Acreage: 1,640,960

Banff, perhaps Canada's premier tourist magnet, attracts millions of visitors every year with its mountains, valleys, glaciers, forests, alpine meadows, lakes and wild rivers along the Alberta flank of the Continental Divide. The park contains at least 25 peaks which tower 9800 feet or more. The blue-green Lake Louise, with glacier-clad Mount Victoria is one of the park's most popular stopping places. The park stretches for nearly 120 miles (193 kilomters), running from Mount Sir Douglas at 11,174 feet (3406 meters) on the south to its common border with Jasper National Park on the north. Yoho National Park, about half Banff's length, lies to the west. The common boundary is the crest of the Canadian Rockies. The two parks are connected by highways over Kicking Horse Pass, elevation 5399 feet (1636 meters) and Vermillion Pass, elevation 5376 feet (1639 meters).

The Canadian Pacific Railway played an important role in the establishment and development of Canada's first national park. In 1883 CPR employees discovered the Cave and Basin Hot Springs at Banff Station. The fledgling railway needed business, and a well-advertised attraction such as a resort park in the Canadian Rockies was just the thing to draw visitors. Recognizing the commercial value of the springs,

rough bathhouses were soon constructed. Two years later a small area was designated the Banff Hot Springs Reserve, modelled after the American one in Hot Springs, Arkansas, with bathhouses being leased.

Both the government and the CPR recognized the springs as a major attraction. The scenic beauty of the surrounding country inspired the Canadian government to protect the area for the enjoyment of all. Following the model of Yellowstone National Park in the United States, which had been created 15 years earlier, the area was set aside as Rocky Mountains Park, later renamed Banff National Park.

A diversity of wildlife abounds in Banff National Park. A total of 53 species of mammals, ranging in size from the pygmy shrew to the grizzly bear, inhabit the park. Other species include red squirrel, beaver, muskrat, moose, white-tailed and mule deer, caribou, mountain goats, coyotes, wolves and mountain lions. Among the bird population are ospreys and bald and golden eagles. Four of the most commonly seen resident birds are members of the crow family—gray jay, Clark's nutcracker, black-billed magpie, and raven. The lakes and rivers of Banff are filled with whitefish, three species of trout, lake chub, black-nosed dace and five-spined stickleback.

The cool climate of Banff best supports coniferous trees, and among the most common are lodgepole pine, white and Engelmann spruce, subalpine fir and Douglas fir. Dense stands of trembling aspen are found in the dry, open areas.

Facing page: Vermilion Lakes, with snow-capped Mount Rundle looming in the distance.

Below: Park visitors marvel at the bright blue waters of Peyto Lake. The color of the park lakes vary from season to season, based on the amount of sediment washed down from the glaciers.

Far right: The town of Banff lies in the shadow of majestic Mount Rundle.

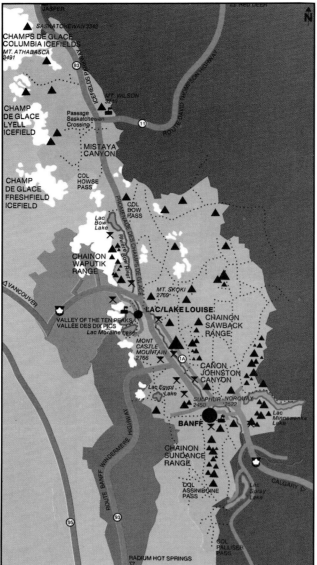

Below: Hiking through the Valley of Ten Peaks is an exhilarating experience.

Bryce Canyon, Utah

Established: 1928   Acreage: 35,835

Bryce Canyon National Park is located in south-central Utah, due north of the Grand Canyon. Paiute Indians described this region as 'Red rocks standing like men in a bowl-shaped canyon.' The many shapes and forms in stone have conjured up all sorts of images: walls and windows, minarets, gables, pagodas, pedestals and temples. It is not known when the land was first seen by white men. James Andrus and his party passed through the area in 1866, and there is little doubt that other parties had also seen Bryce Canyon but their reports escaped notice.

Bryce Canyon is not a canyon at all, but a spectacular amphitheater carved by erosion by water in the 50 to 60 million-year-old rocks of the Pink Cliffs. These cliffs are the uppermost step in the Grand Staircase that rises to the north between Grand Canyon and Bryce Canyon National Parks. The staircase is a series of cliffs, all retreating to the north as the super-imposed rock layers of southern Utah are eroded. The capstone of the Grand Staircase is the Pink Cliffs (9100 feet)—ancient lake deposits once more than 2000 feet thick, but now eroded away to 800 to 1300 feet.

The tallest cliffs among the steps of the Grand Staircase are the White Cliffs (2200 feet), which are really tan in color but look white in sunlight. The Vermilion Cliffs are a brilliant, dark red and can be seen while either walking through Zion Canyon or driving along the road to the Grand Canyon. Near the south entrance to the park are the rocks of the Chocolate, or Belted, Cliffs. From sunrise to sunset, the visitor is dazzled by vivid color. The reds and yellows are caused by iron oxide in the rocks, the purples and lavenders by manganese.

The forests and meadows of Bryce Canyon are home to a wide range of animal species. At the bottom of the food chain is a large rodent population—chipmunks, ground squirrels, prairie dogs, mice, gophers and other species—that feed on seeds and nuts. These small mammals are preyed upon by badger, skunk, bobcat, weasel, ring-tailed cat, gray fox and coyote.

Below: Fairyland Canyon, with the Sinking Ship formation in the background (left).

Mule deer are the largest species of mammals that roam Bryce Canyon. Gone now are the large mammals that once existed here—grizzly bear and timber wolf—and many more are rare—elk, cougar, bighorn sheep, and blond bear. Man has wiped out their numbers, and, sadly, the park is not large enough to offer adequate protection for these vanishing species.

*A wonderful way to experience the natural beauty of Bryce is to hike along the trails. The Chinese Wall (**left**) is just one of the many spectacular sights along the Fairyland Loop Trail.*

Right: *Breathtaking rock formations along the Fairyland Loop Trail.*

Below: *Sunrise Point is one of the best places in the park to behold the awesome beauty and grandeur of the pinnacles and spires.*

Canyonlands, Utah

Established: 1964   Acreage: 337,570

Canyonlands is located in southeastern Utah in the heart of the Colorado Plateau. Wind and water have cut flat layers of sedimentary rock into hundreds of colorful canyons, mesas, buttes, fins, arches and spires. In the center are two large canyons carved by the Green and Colorado Rivers. Surrounding the river are three very different regions of the park: to the north, Island in the Sky; to the west, the Maze; and to the east, the Needles.

Island in the Sky serves as Canyonlands' observation tower, a high, broad mesa (6000-6500 feet) connected to the 'mainland' by a narrow piece of land. Near the mesa's edge is White Rim, an almost continuous sandstone bench 1200 feet below the island, and beneath the shadow of the rim are the rivers. Perhaps the strangest geologic feature on Island in the Sky is Upheaval Dome (1500 feet), which looks more like a meteor crater or volcanic caldera than a dome, and, in fact, one theory suggests that the dome was created when a meteor hit.

One of the most remote regions in the United States, the Maze district is Canyonlands' wildest region. The maze itself is a jumble of canyons that has been described as a '30 square mile puzzle in sandstone.' Beyond are the oddly shaped walls, buttes, mesas and towers of the Land of Standing Rocks,

the Dollhouse and the Fins. Few people had ventured into the canyons before it was established as a national park, and even today less than 8000 people visit each year.

The Needles district is so named because of the fantastically shaped and beautifully colored rock formations— arches, rock spires, canyons, potholes. The diversity of names in the Needles reflects the diversity of the land itself. Devil's Kitchen and Angel Arch. Elephant Hill and Caterpillar Arch. Gothic Arch and Paul Bunyan's Potty. The dominant landforms are the Needles themselves, naked rock pinnacles banded in orange and white. The wildly beautiful rock formations were chiseled out of the bedrock by the forces of wind, water and ice.

Prehistoric Indian ruins and pictographs are densely concentrated here. This was once the land of the Anasazi Indians—the Ancient Ones. Here they grew corn, squash and beans; hunted deer and bighorn; and gathered seeds, fruits and roots. Many of their stone and mud dwellings and storehouses still remain, as do the petroglyphs they etched on the cliff walls.

Even the rivers reflect the wild, isolated character of the park. The 14 miles of rapids through the Cataract Canyon are among the most treacherous white water stretches in the United States. As the only major source of water in a dry expanse, the rivers draw deer, fox, beaver, bobcat and migratory birds, which find shelter in the riverside cottonwoods, tamarisks and willows. Lush hanging gardens of maidenhair fern, monkey flower and columbine cling to the high cliffs.

Right: *Canoeing the quiet upper waters of the Green River through Labyrinth Canyon.*

Below: *View of Island in the Sky from Meander Canyon along the Colorado River.*

Above: The Maze—heart of the wild and primitive Canyonlands—is one of the most and inaccessible regions in the United States.

Right: The aptly named waters of the Stillwater Canyon on the Green River. When the Green River meets the Colorado River, these still waters become a raging river, rushing and tumbling through the 14-mile (23-kilometer) rapids of Cataract Canyon.

Capitol Reef, Utah

Established: 1971   Acreage: 241,904

The Navajo Indians called it the 'Land of the Sleeping Rainbow' — a strange, but beautiful, country where colors of the rainbow can be seen in the many rock layers. Capitol Reef was so rugged and remote that it remained almost untouched by white settlers until the late 1800s. It resembled an ocean reef around a tropical island—difficult to cross. The term 'reef' as applied to land formations means a ridge of rock that is a barrier. This reef was named for one of its high points, Capitol Dome, which looks like the dome of the US Capitol.

Capitol Reef National Park is located on the Colorado Plateau. As the area began rising to its present heights toward the end of the age of dinosaurs, pressures on the rock increased as the plateau rose, and resulted in a 100-mile long formation called the Waterpocket Fold. Considered unique by geologists because of its great size, it is the main reason for the establishment of the park. As the rock was folding, it was also eroding, creating the cliff faces, arches, monoliths and canyons one sees today.

The lush vegetation along the fertile plains of the Fremont River provides a stark contrast to the barren cliffs and terraces. Cottonwoods and willows grow along the riverbanks, but plant life exists in the drier parts of the park as well. Hardy pinyon jay, pinyon pine and Utah juniper live in the dry sandstone of the terraces. The sandy floor, piles of rock debris and water-worn holes on the canyon walls are home to side-blotched lizard, antelope squirrel and canyon wren. After a rain, pockets of rain remain, forming a temporary home for shrimp and spadefoot tadpoles. By the time the water dries, the tadpoles have progressed through their life cycles and become toads.

Human beings inhabited the Capitol Reef area as long ago as 800 AD. The Fremont Indians lived along the Fremont River for about 400 years. Their petroglyphs seem to indicate hunting, because they show desert bighorn sheep and figures of people. Some of their stone tools and storage bins—moki huts—still exist in the park. Later, Paiute Indians passed through Capitol Reef, hunting game and gathering food, but humans would not live in the area again until the Mormons settled there in 1880. The tiny town of Fruita, as the Mormon community was called, was widely known for its orchards—which are now protected by the National Park Service as a historic landscape.

Below: The rugged cliffs of Capital Reef offer a striking contrast to the orchards below.

Left: The sharply curving Goosenecks of Sulphur Creek. This rugged land presents a challenge to the experienced hiker.

Right: Capitol Reef National Park got its name from the rugged landscape that, like a reef around a tropical island, was a barrier to travel. The white sandstone domes reminded the early settlers of the US Capitol in Washington, DC.

Below: The jagged ridges and rounded domes create a dazzling display of vivid color, never to be forgotten.

Glacier, British Columbia

Established: 1886   Acreage: 330,440

In both Glacier and Mount Revelstoke a distinctive topography has formed. Massive, angular mountains and steep-walled valleys characterize the Columbia Mountains, distinguishing them from the younger Rockies to the east. Glacier National Park's ice-covered peaks, sheer mountain walls, avalanche-scarred valleys and huge sheets of perpetual ice represent some of the most striking mountain terrain in the world. The heavy snowfalls maintain more than 400 glaciers in the park, and a blanket of ice and snow covers about 12 percent of the park area year round. Even during the summer, snow may fall high in the mountains.

Providing a stark contrast to the snowy mountaintops are the dense rainforests of the valleys. Devil's club, thimbleberry, false box and luxuriant ferns create an impenetrable jungle. Here, too, grow the giant western red cedar, western hemlock and western yew. In the valley live black bear, Stellar's jays and ravens. Farther up the mountainside, the cedars and hemlocks are replaced by subalpine fir and Engelmann spruce, which harbor gray jays, blue grouse and red squirrels. In the upper reaches of the subalpine, the forests thin and the wildflowers cover the countryside with a wild display of color. Gradually the temperatures grow colder and the soil becomes too thin to support a forest. This is the alpine tundra—a starkly beautiful and raw wilderness.

In a century of searching, surveyors have located only one likely route across the Selkirk range of the Columbias: Rogers Pass. Without this pass, all railways and highways would have to take a lengthy detour northward around the mountains by following the Big Bend of the Columbia River. In 1871, British Columbia joined Canada with the understanding that a transcontinental railway would soon be constructed to link it to the east. The rails had stretched across the prairies and were aimed at the heart of the mountains awaiting a link between Calgary and Vancouver. By 1885, after months of trial by avalanche, forest fire and rainstorm, the Canadian Pacific Railway had crossed Rogers Pass and Canada's first transcontinental railway became a reality.

When the first passenger trains ran through the pass in the summer of 1886, the Canadian Government took steps to preserve the area for all time. CPR's General Manager, Cornelius Van Horne, described the area as 'the climax of mountain scenery.'

Right: The red squirrel—or pine squirrel—is one of Glacier's smallest inhabitants.

Far right: Steller's jays can be found year round in the interior rainforest of Glacier National Park. These rugged individualists will eat just about anything—grain, insects, fruits and seeds.

Right: The image of the spectacular snow-covered peaks and steep walls of the Columbia Mountains will be forever etched in the memory of this visitor to Glacier.

Facing page: Hard to believe, but the huge, ambling grizzly bear can run as swiftly as a race horse. Visitors to the park often do not realize how particularly vicious these bears are.

Glacier, Montana

Established: 1910   Acreage: 1,013,595

Much of Glacier is a pristine wilderness with a myriad of wildflowers and wildlife, along with spectacular mountain ranges with sculptured glacial valleys, ice cold lakes, alpine meadows and prairie grasslands. Dense forests of larch, spruce, fir and lodgepole pine exist with western red cedar and western hemlock. Alpine areas display beargrass, heather and glacier lily, while the prairie boasts pasque flower, shooting star and Indian paintbrush.

Roaming through this exquisite environment are bighorn sheep, mountain goats, moose, elk and grizzly and black bears. *Audubon Magazine* reports Glacier Park as having the densest grizzly population in North America—one bear to every eight square miles compared to one bear per 40 square miles in Yellowstone and one bear per 57 square miles in Alaska's Brook Range. Species of birds include the osprey, water ouzel, ptarmigan, Clark's nutcracker, thrushes and the endangered bald eagle. Each fall kokanee salmon and bald eagles arrive at McDonald Creek—the salmon to spawn and the eagles to feed on the salmon.

These elements make up Glacier National Park in the United States and the adjoining Waterton Lakes National Park

in Canada. Divided by the international boundary, the parks are united in the most natural ways. The Upper Waterton Valley, carved by glaciers, lies in both countries; the native plants and animals are similar; and the massive Rocky Mountains span both nations. In recognition of this, the US Congress and the Canadian Parliament established them as the first International Peace Park in the world in 1932. Though the parks are operated independently, there is a great deal of routine cooperation between the personnel on a day-to-day basis.

Visitors to the park can enjoy hiking and camping, swimming and boating, biking and horseback riding amidst the scenic beauty of Glacier National Park. In addition to 1000 miles of trails, a number of roads covering 300 miles ease the access through this breathtaking park. The famed Going-to-the-Sun Road (50 miles) was put under contract in 1925 and completed in 1932. A triumph in highway engineering, more than 60 percent of the excavation for this roadway was through solid rock and accomplished with hand tools. From west to east, the road skirts Lake McDonald, then climbs to the higher country along the Garden Wall, crosses the Continental Divide at Logan Pass (6646 feet), and descends to St Mary Lake.

Among Glacier's Continental Divide peaks there is one small peak with a unique characteristic. From its side, flow three creeks, named Atlantic, Pacific and Hudson Bay. Each

Facing page: During the harsh winters, bighorn sheep cluster together near Many Glacier.

Below: *The unspoiled wilderness of the mountain ranges and crystal clear blue lakes of Glacier National Park in Montana.*

of these streams, which head within yards of one another, flows into the body of water bearing the same name. Hudson Bay Creek flows into Red Eagle Creek and eventually the St Mary River, which in turn flows north into Canada. Atlantic Creek flows into the North Fork of Cut Bank Creek, then the Marias River and finally the Missouri, 11 miles downstream from Fort Benton, Montana. Pacific Creek flows into Nyack Creek, then the Middle Fork of the Flathead and eventually the Columbia River in the state of Washington.

Nestled between Norris Peak to the north and Razoredge to the south lies the appropriately named Triple Divide Peak. On its east side is Mount James, which is the beginning of the Hudson Bay Divide. Other peaks in this range are Amphitheater, Medicine Owl, Kakitos and Divide.

In addition to the park's many campgrounds, visitors can avail themselves of accomodations on the other end of the spectrum in the form of rustic, yet large and well appointed grand hotels. These lodges, located at the East Glacier (The Glacier Park Lodge), Lake McDonald and Many Glacier were constructed of huge native Cedar logs by the Great Northern Railroad and completed in 1912. A fourth lodge at Rising Sun on St Mary Lake was destroyed by fire 30 years later, and the others were sold in 1960 to an independent operator—the Glacier Park Company—who also operates other visitor facilities within Glacier as well as the Prince of Wales Hotel in adjacent Waterton Lakes National Park.

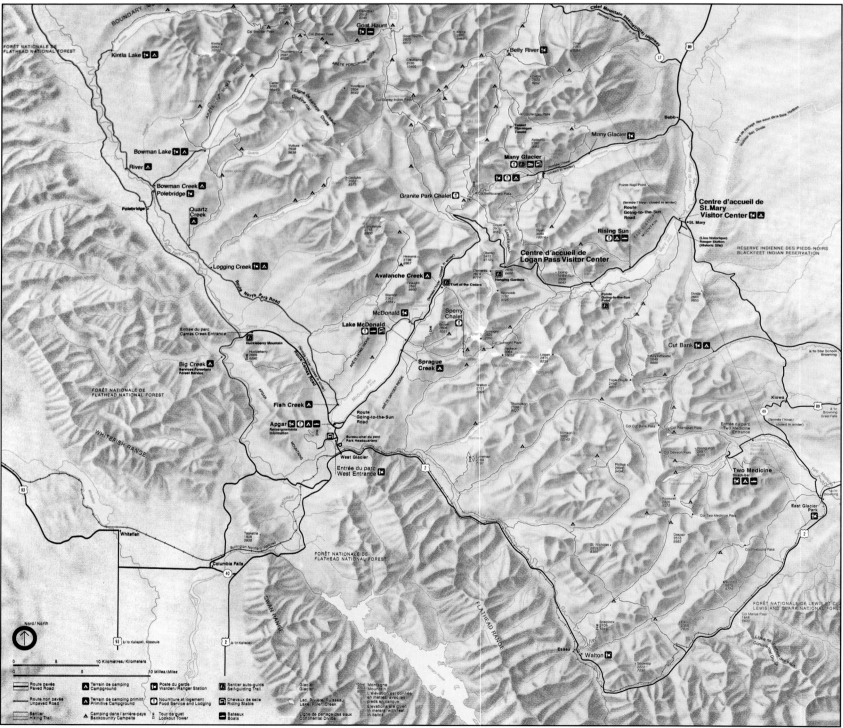

Above left: *St Mary Lake, framed by the awe-inspiring Rocky Mountains.*

Above: *Rising 8774 feet (2674 meters) above sea level, Mount Clements towers over Logan Pass on the Continental Divide in Glacier National Park.*

Right: *Though these bear cubs and their mother may appear to be a unique photo opportunity, they are wild animals and should be avoided. Grizzlies are potentially dangerous.*

Grand Teton, Wyoming

Established: 1929   Acreage: 310,516

Towering more than a mile above the floor of the valley known as Jackson Hole, the Grand Teton rises to 13,770 feet above sea level. Seven Teton peaks reach above 12,000 feet. In contrast to the abrupt eastern face, the west side of the range slopes gently, showing the angle of tilt of this block resulting from the faulting process that created these mountains. Because of the way the mountains formed, no foothills hide jagged peaks and broad canyons.

More than any other erosional force, mountain glaciers of the last major glacial period shaped the Teton skyline. Upon leaving narrow canyons, the larger glaciers spread onto the valley floor, while melting at a speed equal to their flow. A huge volume of unsorted rock formed natural dams. These now encompass Leigh, Jenny, Taggart, Bradley and Phelps lakes.

The geologic forces and natural systems that interact to produce the inspiring scenery also nurture a remarkable diversity of animals. During the summer months, nearly 3000 elk migrate to the park, where they gain enough weight to sustain them through the harsh winter months. A few inches of snow triggers their return to the National Elk Refuge south of the park. A small herd of buffalo also summer in the park. Moose, pronghorn, coyote, black bear, and even an occasional grizzly are found in the river bottomlands, sagebrush flats and canyons.

Historically, Jackson Hole was a buffer zone between territories claimed by various Indian tribes, such as the Shoshone, Gros Ventre, Flathead, Blackfeet and Sheepeaters. The harsh winters prevented any one tribe from living there year round. Fur trappers were the first white men to explore the Teton Country—John Colter was probably the first. With the decline of the fur trade in the late 1830s, Jackson Hole was forgotten until the military and civilian surveys of the 1860s and 1870s rediscovered the region. By the late 1800s, Jackson Hole had acquired a reputation for its splendid hunting and fishing, and soon tourism flourished. In 1925, Pierce Cunningham, a local rancher, circulated a petition calling for the preservation of the area and the wildlife that inhabited it. Four years later much of the Teton range was protected with the establishment of a national park. Following years of debate, Congress added the Jackson Hole portion in 1950.

Facing page: The majestic peaks of the Tetons create a dramatic skyline.

Below: The clear blue waters of the mountain lakes mirror the Tetons, doubling their prominence.

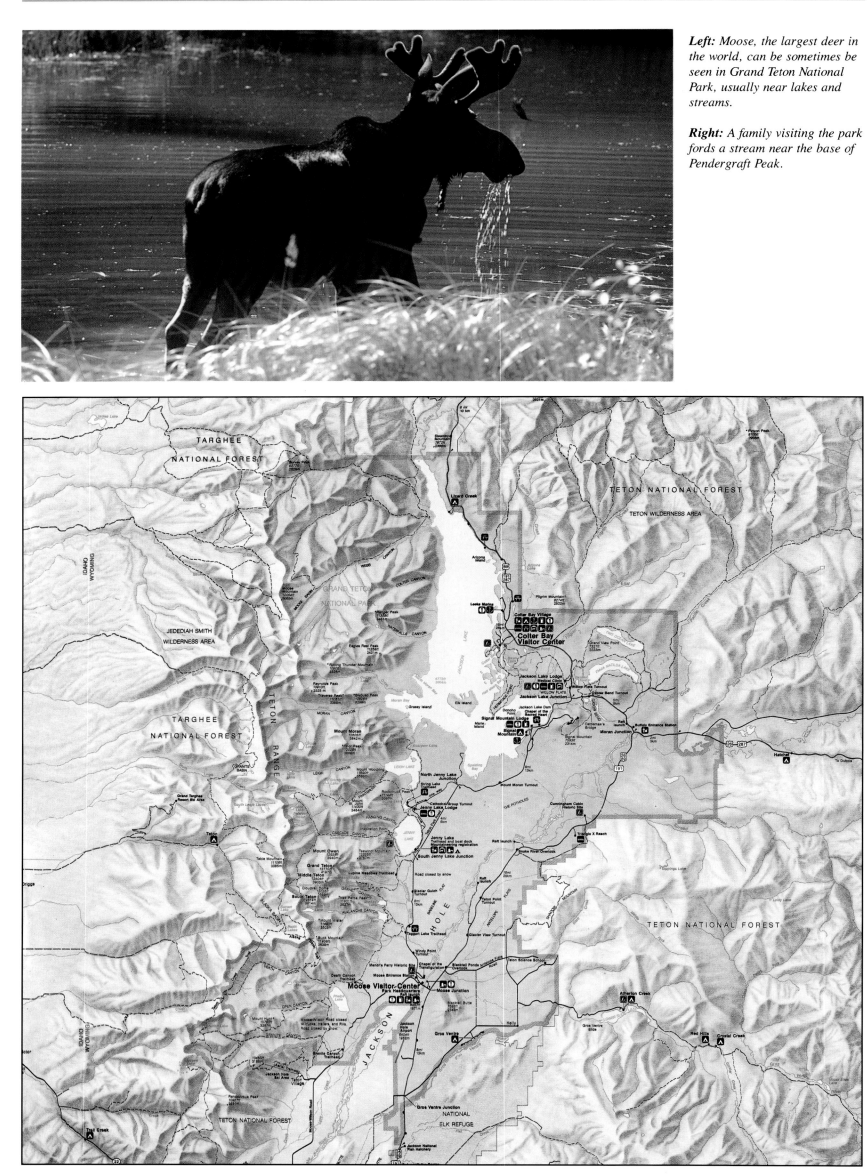

Left: Moose, the largest deer in the world, can be sometimes be seen in Grand Teton National Park, usually near lakes and streams.

Right: A family visiting the park fords a stream near the base of Pendergraft Peak.

Jasper, Alberta

Established: 1907   Acreage: 2,688,000

The largest of Canada's Rocky Mountain national parks, Jasper spans broad valleys and rugged mountains along the eastern slopes of the Rockies. The mountains were created millions of years ago on the floor of a great inland sea, and layers of sedimentary rock of the sea bed were pushed up and folded by forces deep beneath the crust of the earth, leaving long, parallel rows of mountains. Today, this mountain landscape consists of glaciers, rivers, lakes, forests and alpine meadows, where a wide variety of exquisite wildflowers thrive during the summer.

The park is home to bighorn sheep, elk, mountain goat and both black and grizzly bears. During much of the year, mule deer, elk and moose inhabit the lower slopes and meadows, along with the smaller mammals, such as the coyote and marten. Wildlife has been known to venture into the streets of the village of Jasper. The bird population at Jasper is smaller than on the wetter, western side of the Rockies. Gray jay, raven and magpie are most commonly seen, but eagles, pipit and ptarmigan are found at the higher altitudes.

The human history of the park includes stories of Indians, fur traders, geologists, railroad surveyors, mountaineers, naturalists and prospectors. Transient campsites and workshops nearly 3000 years old have been uncovered in the park, but no permanent camps have been found, perhaps because wildlife was scarce in the past. The first white explorers ventured into the Jasper region in the early 1800s in search of a trade route across the mountains. With the coming of the Grand Trunk Pacific Railway line through the Yellowhead Pass in 1907, the federal government decided to preserve the area as a national park. A local trading post operated by Jasper Hawse provided the inspiration for the park's name.

Today, many of the park's striking features—the Athabasca Glacier, Sunwapta and Athabasca Falls and Miette Hotsprings—are accessible by road. Visitors can drive a switchback road right to the base of one of the highest peaks in the area, the glacier-covered Mount Edith Cavell. Visitors can also ride the Jasper Tramway on Whistler Mountain—the easiest way to see life above the timberline. A spectacular gorge—the deeply-gouged Maligne Canyon—and the brilliant beauty of glacial-fed Maligne Lake are just some of the many attractions.

Above right, top: The rugged, snow-covered peaks of the Morning Sentinels in Jasper National Park.

Canoeing on Pyramid Lake (above right, center) is a popular summertime activity in the park. In the winter, park visitors enjoy cross country skiing (right).

Facing page: The essence of perfection—snow-covered Medicine Lake in winter.

Kootenay, British Columbia

Established: 1920   Acreage: 340,480

Kootenay National Park, on the west slope of the Continental Divide, offers the chance to compare mountains of the Main and Western Ranges of the Rocky Mountains and observe the headwaters of the Kootenay River. It is a land of startling contrasts—towering summits and hanging glaciers, narrow chasms and color-splashed mineral pools.

The park's mixture of landscape and human history captures the visitor's attention: Marble Canyon Nature Trail offers the chance to closely examine the effect of water erosion on the earth's surface; nearby are ochre-tinted paint pots which were once used by the Kootenay Indians to make vermilion paint to decorate their bodies and tepees. The Redwall Fault, marked by scattered rock and red cliffs, has its own fascination, while Radium Hot Springs, the site of the legendary Indian spirit Nipika, is a natural mineral spring heated deep in the earth's crust.

Since prehistoric times, this part of the central Canadian Rockies served as a major north-south traffic route, and Indians met at the hot springs long before fur traders and explorers crossed the area's challenging mountain passes. Today the Banff-Windermere Highway, stretching from north to south through the park, is filled with views of wildlife and stunning geographical features. The park's many trails lead visitors through alpine meadows to mountain lakes and snowfields.

Far right: Elk can often be observed at the Animal Licks, usually at dawn or dusk.

Facing page: Bighorn rams high in the grassy meadows of Kootenay National Park.

Below: A frozen waterfall provides a wondrous backdrop for these snowshoers in Haffner Canyon.

Mesa Verde, Colorado

Established: 1906   Acreage: 52,085

Mesa Verde National Park preserves a spectacular remnant of the Anasazi Indians' 1000-year-old culture. For over 700 years their descendents lived and prospered here, eventually building elaborate stone cities in the sheltered recesses of the canyon walls. In the late 1200s, within the span of one or two generations, they abandoned their homes and moved away.

Although they left no written records, their ruins tell of a people adept at building, artistic in their basket-making and skillful at wresting a living from a difficult land. The Anasazi built their dwellings under the overhanging cliffs using sandstone as their basic construction material. The sandstone was shaped into rectangular blocks the size of a loaf of bread. The mortar between these blocks was a mix of mud and water. Rooms averaged six by eight feet, just enough space for two or three people.

Much of the daily routine took place in the open courtyards in front of the rooms. The women made pottery there, while the men made tools—knives, axes, awls and scrapers—out of stone and bone. Farming, however, occupied most of their time. They supplemented their crops of corn, beans and squash by gathering wild plants and hunting deer, rabbits and squirrels. The Anasazi grew crops and hunted on the mesa tops, which were fertile and well-watered except in times of drought. They reached their fields by climbing up hand-and-toe-hold trails carved out of the cliff walls.

By 1300 Mesa Verde was deserted. The last quarter of the century was a time of drought and crop failures. When the Anasazi left, they may have travelled south into New Mexico and Arizona. Whatever happened, it is likely that some Pueblo Indians today are descendents of the cliff dwellers of Mesa Verde.

Far right: Square Tower House, a powerful reminder of the Anasazi—the Ancient Ones—who built these impressive cliff dwellings during the 1200s.

Below: Spruce Tree House was named for the tall spruce tree growing in front of the dwelling.

Above: A close-up of Spruce Tree House. Note the size of the sandstone bricks.

Left: The tower section of Cliff Palace. Discovered by chance in December 1888, Cliff Palace is the largest ruin in the park.

Mount Revelstoke, British Columbia

Established: 1914   Acreage: 64,896

Mount Revelstoke, a majestic and unspoiled national park, offers a unique perspective on mountain contrasts. The slow and scenic drive on Summit Road leads from the Columbia Forest—a dense rainforest of giant cedar, hemlock, white pine and Devil's club—through subalpine forest to meadows where scarlet Indian paintbrush, white valerian, yellow arnica and blue lupine create a kaleidoscope of colors.

From the summit of Mount Revelstoke, there is an excellent view of the ice-clad peaks of the Monashee Range, and the sharp peaks of the Selkirk Ranges line the eastern horizon. Below are the valleys of the Columbia and Illecillewaet rivers.

Hiking in the park's trails gives summer visitors the chance to explore a variety of lifezones in the Columbia Mountains. A short, easy hike along Mountain Meadows Trail leads through a wildflower area to a crevice named 'The Icebox.' Giant Cedars Trail winds through a stand of red cedars nearly 1000 years old. Trails to Eva, Miller and Jade lakes are longer, more challenging hikes, and offer fishing in subalpine water. In winter, the deep and lasting snow lets visitors enjoy cross country skiing and snowshoeing.

Above right: *A yellow-bellied marmot suns itself on a rocky ledge in Mount Revelstoke National Park.*

Right: *The imposing Selkirks once seemed an insurmountable barrier to the west.*

Above: For a few short weeks each summer, the mountainsides are drenched in a bright display of color.

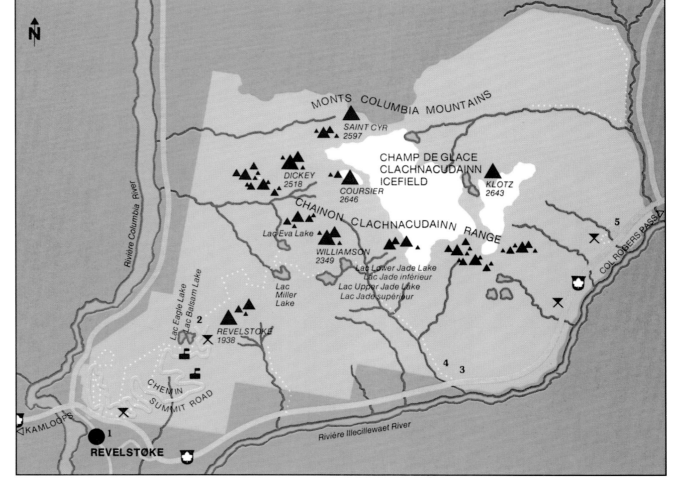

MONTS COLUMBIA MOUNTAINS

SAINT CYR
2597

CHAMP DE GLACE
CLACHNACUDAINN
ICEFIELD

DICKEY
2518

COURSIER
2646

KLOTZ
2643

CHAINON CLACHNACUDAINN RANGE

Lac Eva Lake

WILLIAMSON
2349

Lac Lower Jade Lake
Lac Jade inférieur
Lac Upper Jade Lake
Lac Jade supérieur

5

COL ROGERS PASS

Lac Eagle Lake

Lac Balsam Lake

Lac
Miller
Lake

2

REVELSTOKE
1938

Rivière Columbia River

CHEMIN
SUMMIT ROAD

4   3

KAMLOOPS

1

REVELSTOKE

Rivière Illecillewaet River

127

Rocky Mountain, Colorado

Established: 1915   Acreage: 266,944

The snow-mantled peaks of Rocky Mountain National Park rise above green alpine valleys and glistening lakes. One third of the park is above the treeline, and here tundra predominates—a major reason why these peaks and valleys have been designated as a national park. As the elevation changes so does the landscape. At the lower levels, the slopes are graced with ponderosa pine, juniper, Douglas fir, blue spruce, lodgepole pine and groves of aspen. At 9000 feet (2700 meters) Englemann spruce and subalpine fir takeover. The forest glades are filled with wildflower gardens of rare beauty and luxuriance, where the blue Colorado columbine reigns. As the trees disappear, the alpine tundra—a harsh, fragile world—begins. Many of the plants here can also be found in the Arctic. Wildlife, both large and small, can be spotted in the park—beaver, marmots, wapiti (elk), deer, coyotes and bighorn sheep.

After the United States acquired the region through the Louisiana Purchase in 1803, explorers, trappers and adventurers passed near the park area. In 1859, Joel Estes and his son, Milton, topped Park Hill and became the first known white men to see the 'park,' an open, forest-rimmed valley, which now bears the Estes name.

During the 1880s, a mining boom struck in what is now the west side of the park, leading to the creation of Lulu City, Dutchtown and Teller. Only low-grade ore was found, however, and the mines were abandoned. When the automobile finally turned out to be a practical mode of transportation, more and more people visited the area and a movement began to set aside the region as a national park. The efforts of one man—Enos Miller, a naturalist and writer—laid the groundwork for the establishment of this breathtaking park.

Rocky Mountain is a park for hikers—more than 355 miles of trails provide access to the remote sections of the park. For those who prefer to remain in their cars, there is Trail Ridge Road, one of the great alpine highways in the United States. Bear Lake Road is one of the few paved roads in the Rockies leading to a high mountain basin. Old Fall River Road, the original road crossing the mountain, gives an idea of what it was like to cross the mountains in the early days of the automobile. Fishing, camping, horseback riding and skiing are other popular activities in the park.

Above right, top: Long's Peak, the park's highest peak. Major John Wesley Powell and his party made the first successful ascent of the summit in 1868, generating an unbounded enthusiasm for mountain climbing in the area.

Above right, center: Wildflowers bloom in the harsh but fragile world of the alpine tundra.

Right: Bear Lake, nestled amid the stunning scenery of the Rockies. Park visitors can enjoy an easy hike around the lake.

Facing page: Dream Lake, with Hallett Peak rising in the background.

Facing page, top left: The delicate blue columbine adorns the alpine meadows of Rocky Mountain National Park.

Facing page, top right: A young bighorn, the living symbol of the park.

Facing page, bottom: Wildflowers set against the dramatic backdrop of water roaring down the mountainside.

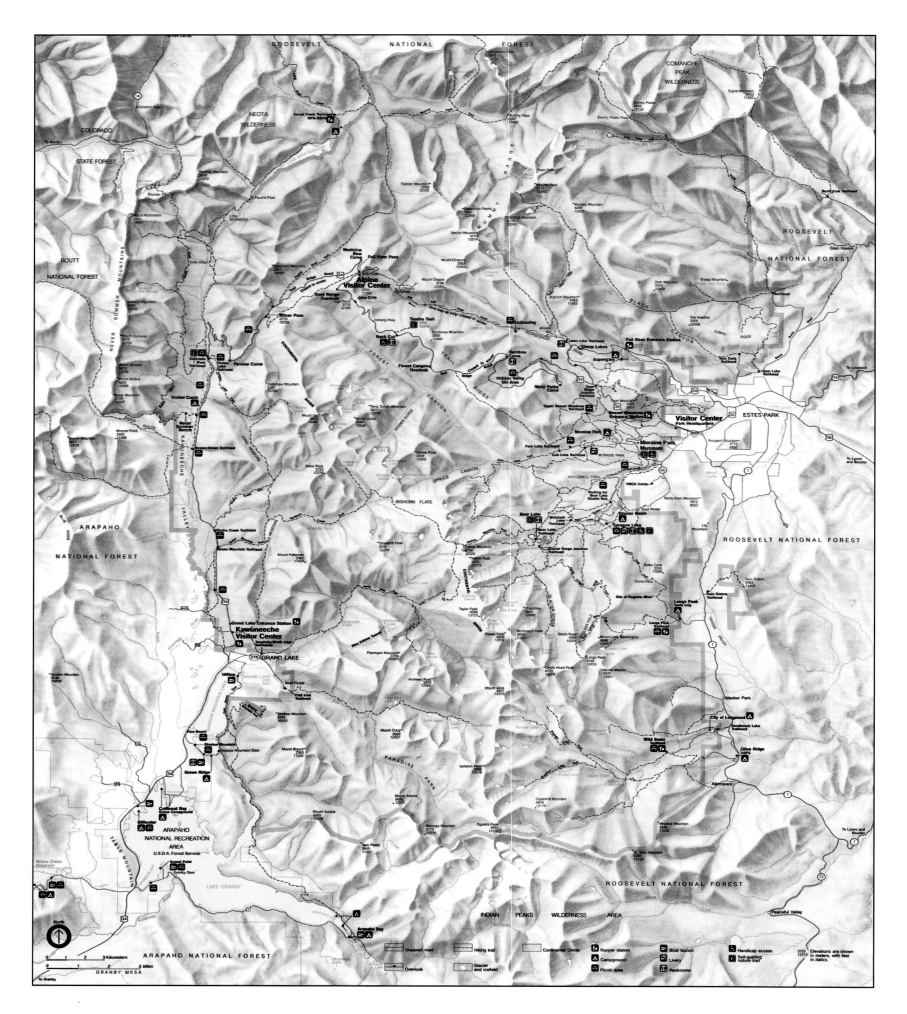

Waterton Lakes, Alberta

Established: 1895   Acreage: 129,920

Described as a place 'where the mountains meet the prairies,' Waterton Lakes National Park occupies a small corner of southwest Alberta. One of the smaller parks in Canada, it was joined with the much larger Glacier National Park in Montana in 1932, forming Waterton-Glacier International Peace Park, a world first.

Glaciation played its part in carving out lakes and re-sculpturing valleys, leaving hanging valleys and waterfalls, and depositing a rolling landscape of glacial moraines (the accumulation of earth and stones), eskers (long, narrow ridges of sand, gravel and boulders) and kames (ridges of stratified drift). The deepest lake in the Canadian Rockies—Upper Waterton Lake—is here. On the international border between the United States and Canada, the lake supports many unusual aquatic organisms, including deepwater sculpin, pygmy whitefish and opossum shrimp. In other parts of the park, the forests, alpine meadows, prairies and marshes support a variety of plants and animals. Elk, mule deer, bighorn sheep, and black and grizzly bears are among the wildlife.

Archaeological sites indicate heavy use of the area in prehistoric times, and when western Canada was settled by white men, the region was shared (in different seasons of the year) by the powerful Blackfoot Nation of the Great Plains and the Kootenay tribes of the Alberta and British Columbia mountains.

Hiking through the forested valleys or delicate alpine meadows offers magnificent views of lakes and peaks. Cruise boats on the lake or a drive through the bison paddock provide another perspective on the scenery. Bus tours, boat rentals and trail rides are other ways to enjoy the striking beauty of Waterton Lakes.

Below: The purple-hued Rockies soar toward the heavens. A third of the park is above the tree line—and here alpine tundra predominates.

Above: The prairie ends abruptly, at the foot of the mountains—a unique feature of the park.

Right: Graceful mule deer abound in Waterton Lakes National Park. The distinctive feature that gives the animal its name is the large, long ears.

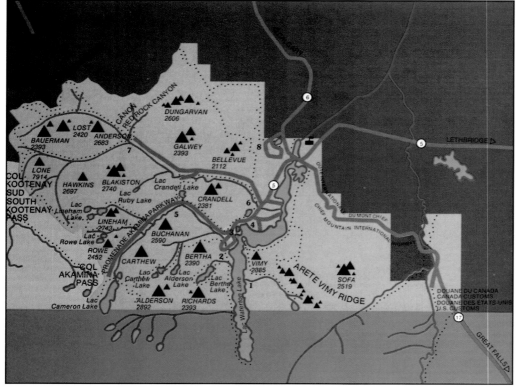

Above: *Winter in Waterton Lakes Valley. Every season has a special beauty.*

Right: *A small group of elk crossing the ice-cold waters of Waterton River.*

Far right: *Vari-colored rocks highlight the Blakiston Valley. The cloud-hidden Canadian Rockies rise in the distance.*

Yellowstone, Wyoming

Established: 1872   Acreage: 2,221,766

The world's first national park—Yellowstone—is located in three states; 96 percent is in Wyoming, three percent in Montana and one percent in Idaho. Yellowstone is a treasure that inspires awe in travellers from around the globe. Although New Zealand and Iceland are known for their geysers, nowhere in the world are there as many active ones as in Yellowstone—200 to 250.

At the heart of Yellowstone's past, present and future is volcanic activity. The magmatic heat from several eruptions, ranging from two million to 600,000 years ago, still powers the park's famous geysers, hot springs, fumaroles and mud pots. Surface water seeps down into porous rock layers to be heated under pressure and then rises back up as geysers or hot springs. Old Faithful is the world's best-known geyser, whose eruption intervals have long varied around an average of 65 minutes. The world's largest geyser, Steamboat, erupts at irregular intervals of days to years.

Yellowstone has the highest concentration of large and small mammals in the lower 48 states, including the American bison, elk, grizzly and black bears, coyotes, bighorn sheep, mule deer, squirrels and marmots. Bird species include osprey, pelican, trumpeter swan and green-wing teal. In addition, Yellowstone is home to 11 species of fish, five species of reptiles and four species of amphibians. The park also boasts a variety of vegetation types, from near-desert vegetation to subalpine meadows and forests. Although the park has 370 miles of paved roads, the best way to enjoy Yellowstone is on the 1000 miles of trails through the backcountry.

Ancient campsites and stone artifacts found in the park indicate that man has lived on the Yellowstone Plateau for most of the 8500 years since the last Ice Age. At the time

Far right: Old Faithful— Yellowstone's most famous geyser. Park visitors count on its regularity, and approximately every hour it delights with an impressive performance of water bursting skyward.

Facing page: The Yellowstone River roars down the falls and through the steep-walled Grand Canyon.

Below: At cliff's edge, a small group of bison stand cloaked in steam.

written records began (a mere 150 years ago), the only Indians living in the park area were a mixed group of Shoshone and Bannock who, lacking the horses and guns necessary to compete with neighboring tribes, had retreated into the mountains to live furtive, impoverished lives. Yellowstone's recent history resonates with colorful tales of fur trappers, miners, surveyors, photographers and artists. The briefly flourishing fur trade in the Rocky Mountains brought such men as John Colter, Jim Bridger and Joe Meek into the area, but a growing scarcity of good furs, along with changing

fashions, ended the fur trade around 1840. Twenty years later, the discovery of gold in Montana brought in exploring parties of miners. In 1869, a different type of exploration, based on curiosity, began. William Henry Jackson's photographs and Thomas Moran's sketches influenced Congress to establish the park, an act which influenced countries throughout the world to preserve their own natural treasures. The disasterous forest fires of 1988 burned one million acres, 1600 square miles of Yellowstone's timberland—nearly half of the park's area.

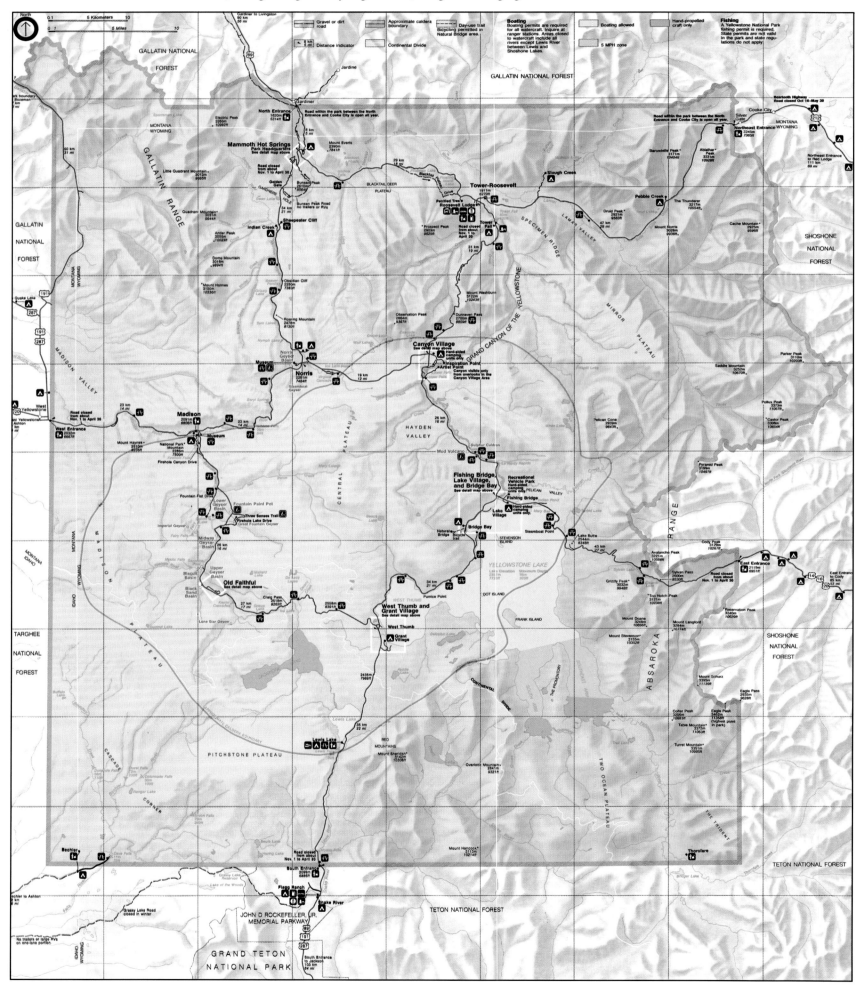

The black bear (**above**) is one of the chief attractions at Yellowstone. Bison (**above right**) can also be spotted in the park.

Right: Mud Volcano. *Yellowstone was born from violent volcanic eruptions that began two million years ago. What is today the park's central basin is the caldera of the latest volcanic eruption—600,000 years ago.*

Far left: Nez Perce Creek gently meanders through Yellowstone Park.

Left: Breathtaking Tower Falls. Tumbling 132 feet, the falls was named for the adjacent volcanic pinnacles.

Overleaf: Morning Glory Pool. Such strange sights as these first drew people to the area. So enthralled were these early visitors that they called for the area to be set aside as a national park—the first in the world.

Below: Osprey Falls—just one of the many wondrous sights in Yellowstone.

*Every year vacationers marvel at Mammoth Hot Springs (**left**) and Old Faithful (**right**).*

__Below:__ The terraces at Mammoth Hot Springs were formed by the steady flow of mineral-laden hot water over thousands and thousands of years.

Yoho, British Columbia

Established: 1886   Acreage: 324,480

'Yoho' is a Cree word expressing awe, and visitors today find the name fitting when they enter Yoho National Park in the heart of the Rocky Mountains. It is an imposing place of lofty peaks, dense forests, glacial lakes and alpine meadows ablaze with wildflowers in the summer.

Hundreds of years ago, Indian tribes established temporary campsites in the park's valleys. Later, in the nineteenth century, the search for the best transportation route through the Rocky Mountain barrier brought the first white men to the area. In 1858 Sir James Hector discovered Kicking Horse Pass, naming it after being kicked and nearly killed by his horse on the site. The Canadian Pacific Railway laid track through the pass in 1884, and since that time the area has been accessible to all.

The mountains that were the curse of railway workers are responsible for the park's many waterfalls, including one of Canada's highest (833 feet) Takakkaw Falls. The green, translucent waters of Emerald Lake and unique geologic features such as the Hoodoos and the natural rock bridge spanning the Kicking Horse River, offer fine subjects for photographers. The Spiral Tunnels on the Big Hill illustrate the danger and excitement of building a railway across the steep west side of the Continental Divide.

Yoho offers many recreational activities. In summer, visitors to the park can camp, hike, swim, backpack, fish and go boating. Winter fun includes cross country skiing and snowshoeing.

Above right: During the summer, the osprey can be spotted soaring above the lakes of Yoho National Park.

Right: Sparkling alpine lakes are nestled high among the rocky peaks of the Continental Divide.

Facing page, top: With its snow-capped mountain peaks, deep silent forests and brilliant turquoise lakes, it is no wonder that Yoho got its name from a Cree word expressing awe.

Far right: The mountain goat makes its home in Yoho's craggy peaks and steep rock faces.

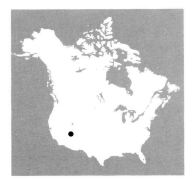

Zion, Utah

Established: 1919   Acreage: 146,551

The names of the trails in Zion—Emerald Pools, Hidden Canyon, Gateway to the Narrows, Canyon Overlook—hint at what can be found beyond the road. The park has a number of surprises, too—a desert swamp, a petrified forest, springs and waterfalls. As with Yellowstone, many scoffed at the first stories of Zion, a wild, rugged country of little-known canyons and plateaus in southern Utah. Nevertheless, the massive, multicolored, vertical cliffs and deep canyons were real.

The centerpiece of the park is Zion Canyon, a narrow, deep (2000 to 3000 foot high walls) canyon with vividly colored cliffs which intimidated the Paiute Indians, who refused to stay here after dark. Along the bottom of the canyon flows the Virgin River, deceivingly powerless in looks, yet this small river carved the rock gorge of Zion Canyon almost singlehandedly. Fremont cottonwoods, willows and velvet ash line the banks of the river, providing a midday refuge from the summer heat for picnickers, as well as for mule deer and many birds. Bobcats, ringtail cats, foxes, rock squirrels and cottontails rest under rocky ledges. The park is also home to mountain lions and mule deer.

Connecting Zion Canyon with the high plateaus to the east is Zion-Mount Carmel Highway, which goes through two tunnels. At one end of the longer tunnel is the Great Arch of Zion, a 'blind' arch carved high in a vertical cliff wall. On the other side of the tunnel is slickrock country. Here rocks colored in white and pastels of orange and red have been eroded into many shapes. The mountains of sandstone known as Checkerboard Mesa provide a fine example of naturally sculpted rock art. In the northwest corner of the park are the Finger Canyons of the Kolob, where the Kolob Canyons Road penetrates the heart of the brilliant red rock country of the steep-walled Finger Canyons. The Kolob has forests of pinyon, jupiter, ponderosa pine, fir and quaking aspen. In winter and early spring, the area is buried under a thick snowpack, which heightens the hues of this already colorful landscape.

In prehistoric times, Zion was inhabited by Basketmakers and Puebloans, and the rainbow canyons once sheltered an ancient race of cave dwellers. When Europeans first discovered the area, the Paiute claimed the region. In 1776, Father Escalante, while on an expedition in the Southwest, chanced upon the Zion region. Fifty years passed before other white men—trappers and fur traders—ventured to Zion. Eventually, the Mormons from Salt Lake City established a small settlement and named the area 'Zion,' meaning 'the heavenly city of God.'

Above right, top: The Narrows of the Zion Canyon. The enormous height of the walls dwarfs the hiker.

Above right, middle: The sheer, vividly colored Watchman towers above the canyon floor.

Facing page: Great White Throne—the symbol of Zion National Park—conveys an overwhelming sense of nobility.

Right: West Temple looms above the Visitor Center in Zion National Park.

THE SOUTHWEST

Big Bend, Texas

Established: 1944   Acreage: 735,416

The Indians said that after making the Earth, the Great Spirit simply dumped all the remaining rocks on the Big Bend. Spanish explorers called it 'the uninhabitable land.' To the casual visitor this may seem true—Big Bend is a land of austere panoramas and open expanses of cactus and scrub brush broken by rugged mountains, towering pinnacles and deeply etched canyons.

The name Big Bend refers to the big U-turn the Rio Grande makes in southwest Texas. The Rio Grande borders the park for 118 miles, in which distance it has carved three major canyons that vary in depth from 1200 to 1500 feet. One of the most startling sights in the park is the teethmarks of beaver on cottonwood or willow trees along the river. The desert heat forces the beavers to live in bank burrows. An oasis for species not adapted to the desert, the river adds to the park's

rich biological complexity. The river flood plain is an area of unparalleled birdwatching. Here brightly colored summer tanagers, painted buntings, vermilion flycatchers and cardinals serve as accent colors to the green foliage. Along the river's gravel and sandbars, visitors can catch sight of birds typically not seen in the desert, such as the sandpiper and killdeer bob.

In 1975, *Science Magazine* reported the discovery of bones in Big Bend National Park of the largest flying creature ever known. According to Douglas Lawson, a doctoral candidate at the University of California, and Dr Wan Langston, director of the Paleontology Laboratory of Vertebrates at the University of Texas, the bones were those of a pterosaur, sometimes called a pterodactyl, a flying reptile with a wing span of 38 feet. This creature became extinct about 60 million years ago.

Big Bend National Park is 97 percent Chihuahuan Desert, one of the four warm North American deserts. This desert is young, about 8000 years old, and is fairly lush, receiving its rainfall during the summer. The desert is commonly per-

Previous pages: The red, rocky cliffs of El Capitan in Guadalupe Mountains National Park.

Above left: The mule deer, the most abundant deer in western North America.

A drive along winding Highway 170 (above right) is one way to experience the rolling, rugged terrain of Big Bend National Park. The more adventurous can try a horseback ride along Window Trail (right).

Facing page: The still waters of Santa Elena Canyon on the Rio Grande River.

ceived as a vast emptiness. On the contrary, the desert is a life zone full of plants and creatures perfectly suited to conditions. The primary plant is the lechuguilla, which appears as a clump of dagger blades protruding from the desert floor. Creosote bushes, for example, produce toxins that discourage other plants from intruding on their growing space, and their leaves are coated with a resin so that they lose little moisture to the air. The wildlife, too, has adapted to the climate. The kangaroo rat never needs to drink because it can metabolize water from the carbohydrates in the seeds it eats.

The Chiso Mountains interrupt the Big Bend country as a green island in a desert sea. During the Paleozoic Era, over 300 million years ago, Big Bend was a sea. The water-covered area, known as the Quachita Trough, extended into what is now Oklahoma and Arkansas. Toward the end of this era, movements buckled the earth's crust to form the mountains.

The mountains, like the river area, are home to animals and plants not found in a desert region. As the Great Ice Age drew to a close and the colder, moister climates retreated northward, many plants and animals became stranded in the cooler Chiso Mountains by the ever-increasing aridity of the surrounding lowlands.

Although it is a wild and untamed land, the region has been known for a long time. Spanish explores were surely among its early white visitors. Old Spanish guns, a sword, some stirrups and other items have been found in park areas.

Hiking is the best way to explore the park, but a river trip down the Rio Grande can be an unforgettable experience. It generally takes six or seven days for a river trip through the park.

Far right and below: The rare beauty of the plants unique to the desert contradicts the commonly held belief that the desert is a barren wasteland.

Carlsbad Caverns, New Mexico

Established: 1930   Acreage: 46,755

In the 1800s settlers discovered Carlsbad Cavern, drawn to it by the spectacle of hundreds of thousands of bats rising up out of the natural entrance in the evening. Not surprisingly, many were skeptical about the natural wonders of this huge, underground wilderness full of unusual cave formations.

The decoration of Carlsbad Cavern with stalactites, stalagmites, helictites and an amazing variety of other formations began over 500,000 years ago, after much of the cavern had been carved out. It happened slowly, drop by drop, at a time when a wetter, cooler climate prevailed. The creation of each formation depended on water that dripped or seeped down into the limestone bedrock and into the cave. Where water dripped slowly from the ceiling, soda straws and larger stalactites appeared. Water falling on the floor created stalagmites. Draperies were hung where water ran down a slanted ceiling.

Carlsbad Caverns is a sanctuary for about 300,000 Mexican free-tail bats. During the day they crowd together on the ceiling of Bat Cave, a passageway near the natural entrance. At night the bats leave the cave in huge swarms. At first a few bats flutter out of the cave, but soon the sky is darkened as a thick whirlwind of bats spiral out the cave. Once out of the cave, the bats fly toward the southeast to feed in the Pecos and Black River valleys. As dawn approaches, the bats head back, individually or in small groups. The bats migrate from Mexico to the caverns every year to give birth and raise their young.

Visitors can tour the underground chambers of the cavern, including the Big Room. Measuring 1800 feet at its longest, 1100 feet at its widest and 255 feet at its highest, the Big Room is one of the world's largest underground chambers. Some other highlights of the tour are crystal clear Mirror Lake and the Bottomless Pit, a black hole 140 feet deep. Above ground, visitors can take the nine and a half mile scenic drive through the dramatic desert landscape or hike along the backcountry trails.

Far right, top: Carlsbad Caverns National Park conducts a number of tours through the dark, vast reaches of the cave.

Far right, middle: The park has thousands of limestone stalactites and stalagmites for visitors to see.

Below: The rock formations of the Chinese Temple impress park vistors with their delicacy.

Above: A walk through the incredible Hall of Giants is a walk through another world.

Right: The Temple of the Sun is one of the most spectacular rock formations in the park.

Grand Canyon, Arizona

Established: 1919 Acreage: 1,218,375

'In the Grand Canyon, Arizona has a natural wonder which, so far as I know, is in kind absolutely unparalleled throughout the rest of the world....Leave it as it is. You cannot improve on it....'

—President Theodore Roosevelt, 1903

The Grand Canyon of the Colorado River is not only awe-inspiring in its depth and mind-boggling in its extent, but it has a dazzling, constantly changing display of colors, light and shadow. Amid this pageantry of color, the Grand Canyon offers panoramic vistas of sunrises and sunsets against the rugged cliffs. It is truly one of the most spectacular sights on the face of the earth. The canyon's statistics are equally amazing: it is about one mile deep; from rim to rim it ranges from 600 feet to 18 miles wide. Measuring all the twists and turns of the river, the canyon is 277 miles long. The canyon's two rims are a five-hour drive apart, but they are also linked by a narrow suspension bridge wide enough for a person and a mule. The North Rim is, on the average, about 1000 feet higher than the South Rim, and the weather is correspondingly cooler and wetter. The North Rim is largely a spruce-fir forest, while the South Rim is drier and its plant life adapted to these conditions.

For those who wish to go below the rim into the canyon itself, mule rides offer an exciting way to view the scenery. Trails along the rims and down into the canyon allow the hiker to experience the canyon from varying perspectives. The canyon can also be viewed from a boat trip on the river.

Four thousand years ago prehistoric Indians lived in the canyon and climbed up steep talus slopes with spears after their dinner of bighorn sheep, spending nights under rock overhangs. Around 500 AD the Anasazi Indians began to move in, hunting and gathering. As they adapted to the environment, they settled down into towns. This phase was called the Pueblo, distinguished by the pottery, granaries and above-ground masonry dwellings. When drought struck about 800 years ago, the Anasazi moved east. Their descendents, the Hopi Indians, now live east of the park.

Wildlife in the park includes part of the largest mule deer concentration in the United States, as well as mountain lions, bobcats, desert bighorn sheep, coyotes and badgers. At Phantom Ranch near the Colorado River are numerous ring-tailed cats. On the North Rim are Kaibab squirrels, and on the South Rim, the Abert squirrels. Both species are beautiful and interesting.

Below: The many-hued Grand Canyon presents a dazzling display of purples, pinks and browns.

Far right: Pima Point on the South Rim affords a spectacular view of the steep walls of the Canyon.

Left: Grand Canyon National Park has a large population of mule deer.

Right: Moran Point, named for Thomas Moran, a painter, who first came to the Grand Canyon with Major John Wesley Powell in the early 1870s.

The park is home to close to 70 species of animals, among them the jackrabbit (below left) and the bighorn sheep (below).

Previous pages: A trip to the Grand Canyon will always be remembered, for it is truly one of the most beautiful places in the world. Seen here is the view from Yaki Point on the South Rim.

Left: Visitors to Grand Canyon National Park will be dazzled by its incredible beauty as well as awed by the sheer size of the Canyon.

The map at right is a detail of the North and South Rim area. The one below shows a detail of Grand Canyon Village.

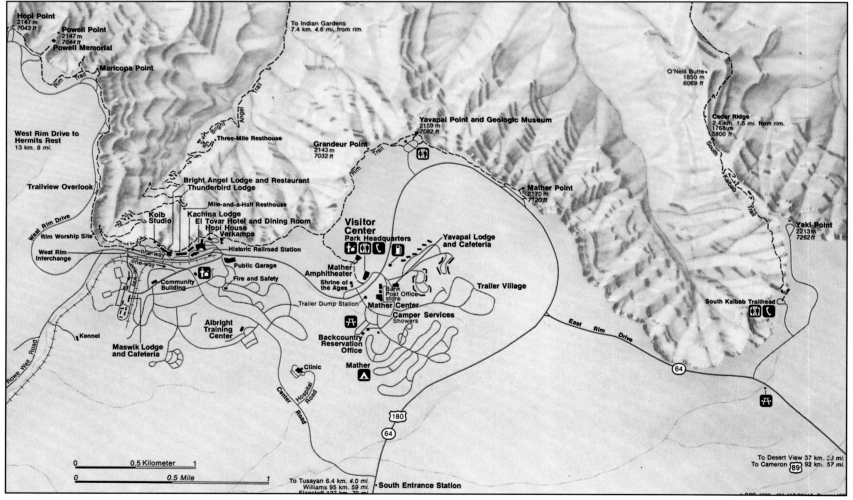

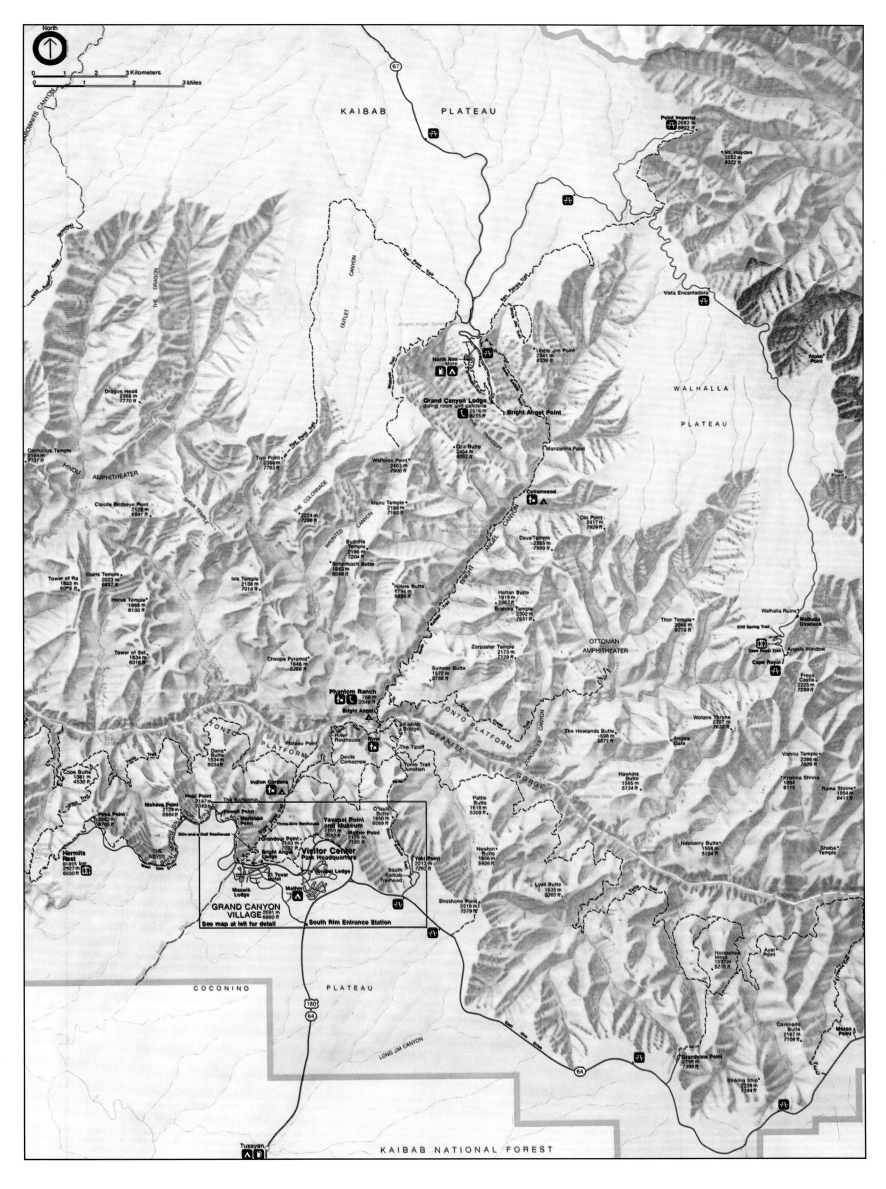

Guadalupe Mountains, Texas

Established: 1972   Acreage: 76,293

The Guadalupe Mountains stand like an island in the desert, silent sentinels watching over the most extensive fossil reef complex known to man. The mountain range resembles a massive wedge—rising in Texas, its arms reach northward into New Mexico. At its 'V' stands El Capitan, a 2000 foot sheer cliff. The park lies astride these mountains' most scenic, rugged portions. The highest point in the Guadalupe Mountains is Guadalupe Peak at 8751 feet (2667 meters). It is also the highest point in the state of Texas.

The Guadalupe Mountains are part of one of the best examples of an ancient marine fossil reef on earth. About 250 million years ago a vast tropical ocean covered the area. Over millions of years, calcareous sponges and algae combined with other lime-secreting marine organisms and large quantities of lime that precipitated directly from the seawater to form the 400-mile long, horseshoe-shaped Capitan Reef. The sea dried up and the reef subsided and was entombed for millions of years, until a mountain-building uplift in the area exposed a part of the fossil reef in the Guadalupes.

For the past 12,000 years the mountain caves, springs, plants and wildlife provided shelter and sustenance to various groups of people. Spanish conquistadors passed near the Guadalupes on trips from Mexico in the late 1500s and found Mescalero Apaches living there. After the mid-1800s came explorers and pioneers whose culture conflicted with that of the Indians. In 1849 the US Army began a campaign against them which lasted for 30 years. Amidst this conflict, Butterfield stagecoaches carried mail through the mountains on the nation's first transcontinental mail route.

At the foot of the Guadalupe Mountains lies the Chihuahuan Desert. Although only a tiny portion of the desert is preserved within the park, its vast, arid plains dominate the views from the mountains. At first glance the desert may appear a barren wasteland, but it is full of life. Agaves, prickly pear cacti, walking-stick callas, yuccas and sotol

thrive in this hot, dry environment. Wildlife prospers too. Lizards, snakes, kangaroo rats, coyotes and mule deer are frequently seen.

The many deep, sheer-sided canyons of the Guadalupe Mountains hold an impressive diversity of plant and animal life, which is perhaps best seen in the McKittrick Canyon. Situated between the desert below and the highlands above, McKittrick has a mix of plants and wildlife found in the desert, canyon woodland and highland forest.

In the mountain high country thrives a dense forest of pine and fir trees, a relic of ancient times, when the climate was cooler and moister. Throughout this wilderness roam mule deer, raccoons, wild turkeys, vultures, mountain lions, black bear and elk. A herd of 50 to 70 elk live in the park, the descendents of animals brought down from Wyoming and South Dakota. The native population was driven to extinction in the early part of this century when man encroached on the elk's territory. Today, the elk within the park are protected from all but natural predators, such as the mountain lion.

Below: The lonesome sound of coyotes barking and howling is a familiar night chorus in the West.

Right: Mule deer live in the desert at the foot of the Guadalupe Mountains as well as in the forests above.

Below: In autumn, the forests of the park are ablaze in bright orange and gold.

Above: Although their numbers have decreased considerably, the mountain lion, or cougar, is the most common cat in North America. Its range extends from British Columbia to western Texas.

Right: In the distance, El Capitan stands proud and ever-watchful over the desert.

Far right: Lush McKittrick Canyon provides a striking contrast to barren El Capitan. (See photo directly to the right.)

Petrified Forest, Arizona

Established: 1962   Acreage: 93,493

Located in northeast Arizona, this high, dry tableland was once a vast flood plain crossed by many streams. To the south, tall, stately pine-like trees grew along the headwaters. Crocodile-like reptiles, huge fish-eating amphibians and small dinosaurs lived among a variety of plants and animals that are known today only as fossils.

About 200 million years ago the tall trees fell and were washed by swollen streams into the floodplain, and were then covered by silt, mud and volcanic ash. This blanket of deposits cut off oxygen and slowed the decay of the logs. Gradually, silica-bearing ground waters seeped through the logs and, little by little, replaced the original wood tissues with silica deposits. The process continued, the silicas hardened and the logs were preserved as petrified wood. The variety of colors in the wood was created by the presence of iron and manganese oxides.

Later, the area sank, was flooded, and covered with freshwater sediments. Afterwards the area was lifted above sea level, which caused the giant logs to crack. Wind and water began to wear away the hardened sediment, exposing the petrified trees and fossilized animal and plant remains. Today the forces of erosion continue to wear down the sediments and reach for the logs and other remains still buried beneath the surface.

A new dimension was added to the Petrified Forest fossil record in 1985 with the discovery of the world's oldest dinosaur skeleton near Chinde Point. Nicknamed Gertie, this plant-eating Plateosaur dates back 225 million years, to the dawn of the Age of Dinosaurs in Triassic times. Although the size of a German shepherd dog, Gertie ranks as an ancestor of the giant brontosaurs.

The Petrified Forest tells the story of human existence as well. In the 1300s, a group of Anasazi Indians lived near the Puerco River in a 76-room pueblo, but Spanish explorers found the place abandoned when they arrived in 1540. In the mid-1800s, US Army mappers and surveyors explored the area and returned East with tales of a remarkable 'painted desert and its trees turned to stone.' Soon ranchers, farmers and sightseers made their way to Arizona. For a time the wood was collected for souvenirs and commercial purposes, but by 1900 local citizens recognized that the supply of petrified wood was not endless and called for the area to be preserved.

Above right: These petrified stumps tell the story of the land long ago, of a time two million years ago when majestic pine trees graced the riverbanks.

Below: Gleaming like quartz, petrified wood, when polished, shows amazing crystal-like patterns.

Right: Logs with root systems still attached tell us that the tree once grew nearby. Generally, many of the trees were washed by the swollen streams into the flood plains and deposited there to be covered by centuries of silt and mud.

Below: As its name suggests, the Painted Desert is a brilliant palette of varying shades of red and white.

THE
FAR WEST

Channel Islands, California

Established: 1980   Acreage: 249,354

Located just off California's southern coast, five of the eight Channel Islands—Anacapa, Santa Cruz, Santa Rosa, San Miguel and Santa Barbara—and their six nautical miles of ocean make up Channel Islands National Park and National Marine Sanctuary. The park and the sanctuary provide a habitat for marine life ranging from the microscopic plankton to the largest creature on earth—the blue whale.

Isolation from the mainland and the mingling of warm and cold water currents in the Santa Barbara Channel help form the Channel Islands' unique character. The plants and animals are similar to those on the mainland, but thousands of years of isolation in unique island environments have resulted in size, shape or color variations among some plants and animals. The island fox, a relative of the mainland's gray fox, is the size of a house cat. It preys on deer mice, which are slightly larger than their mainland counterparts.

Isolation has also protected the islands. Tidepools, unlike those found on the mainland, are brimming with life—sea anemones, abalone, sea urchins, limpets. The undercover rocks at San Miguel are still covered with white-plumed sea anemones, and vivid purple hyprocorals filter water for food near Santa Cruz Island, the largest and most diverse of the park islands.

Seafaring Indians plied the Santa Barbara Channel in swift, seaworthy canoes called tomols. The Chumash, or 'island people,' had villages on the large islands and traded with the mainland Indians. In 1542, explorer Juan Rodriguez entered the same channel, the first European to land on the islands. Beginning in the late 1700s, Russian, British and American fur traders searched the islands' coves and shorelines for sea otters. After the otter was hunted almost to extinction, hunters then concentrated on taking seals and sea lions for their fur and oil.

In the early 1800s the Chumash Indians were removed to the mainland missions. By the mid-1800s, except for the fishermen who operated from cove camps, ranching became the economic mainstay. The Santa Cruz Island ranch produced sheep, cattle, honey, olives and some of the finest early California wines.

Each island is unique, with its own history and topography. Even the flora and fauna can vary from island to island. Santa Cruz Island has eight species of plants not found on any of the other islands. Its diversity of habitat makes Santa Cruz a biologist's paradise.

Previous pages: Beautiful blue Lake Tenaya in Yosemite National Park is rimmed by gently rolling foothills of the Sierra Nevada.

Above right, top: Arch Rock on Anacapa Island. The closest island to the mainland, Anacapa is composed of three small islets—East Anacapa, Middle Anacapa and West Anacapa—that are accessible to each other only by boat. Migrating whales can often be seen in the offshore waters between January and March.

Above right, middle: The lighthouse on East Anacapa Island stands as a reminder of those solitary individuals who, using the lighthouse's bright beacon, warned sailors away from the fog-hidden dangers.

Right: From August to December, the elephant seal lives out in the ocean, feeding on fish and other deepwater marine life. In December, they return to the islands to breed.

Facing page: Except for Frenchy's Cove, the entire island of West Anacapa is closed to protect the nesting area of the brown pelican.

Crater Lake, Oregon

Established: 1902 Acreage: 160,290

Crater Lake, the deepest lake in the US (1932 feet), is located inside Mount Mazama, a once active volcano. Erroneously named when a camping party, led by Jim Sutton, put a boat onto the lake and explored Wizard Island, the lake is not in a crater, but rather sits in a caldera formed by the volcano's collapse.

For half a million years Mount Mazama produced huge eruptions, interrupting long periods of inactivity. Ash, cinder and pumice exploded upward, building the mountain to a height of about 12,000 feet. Satellite cones on Mazama's flanks created today's Mount Scott, Hillman Peak and The Watchman. Glaciers periodically covered Mount Mazama's flanks and carved out the U-shaped valleys, such as Munson Valley and Kerr Notch. About 6800 years ago the climactic eruptions occurred. The Mazama magma chamber emptied and the volcano collapsed, leaving a huge, bowl-shaped caldera in its place. The mountain vanished. It lies scattered over eight states and three Canadian provinces. In the park's Pumice Desert, ash lies 50 feet deep. The explosions were 42 times greater than of Mount St Helen's in 1980.

At first the caldera's floor was too hot to hold water. Renewed volcanism sealed the caldera and built the Wizard Island and Merriam cones, volcanoes in a volcano. After volcanic activity stopped, water began to collect. No stream runs into or out of the lake, so it is considered a closed ecological system.

Originally, Crater Lake contained no fish. Six species were introduced, and of these three remain today: rainbow and brown trout and kokanee salmon. Today, the lake is no longer stocked so that its natural system can be preserved.

Nestled amid rolling mountains, volcanic peaks and evergreen forests, this incredibly blue lake is a breathtaking sight. For much of the year, a thick blanket of snow encircles the lake, creating a winter wonderland. At higher elevations, the snowpack prevents fires and insulates the roots of the mountain hemlocks, which grow to enormous sizes in spite of the short growing season. Also found are shasta red fir and whitebark pine. At the lower levels, ponderosa pine prosper, as do shrubs and wildflowers.

A number of birds and animals inhabit the park. Ravens, jays, nutcrackers, deer, ground squirrels and chipmunks are frequently seen. Present, but seldom seen, are elk, black bear, foxes, porcupines, pine martens, chickaree squirrels and pikas. Hawks, owls, juncos, chickadees and nuthatches make their home in the backcountry. All of these creatures are intertwined in complex relationships with the plant life and natural forces of the land.

Above, far right: This view of Crater Lake shows the Phantom Ship, an unusual rock formation.

Below: An aerial view of Crater Lake. For most of the year, this incredibly blue lake is rimmed by a circle of snow.

Mount Bailey

Red Cone

Hillman Pea

The Watchm

1
Cone-building phase begins

2
Vents

Right: In the midst of the lake, lies Wizard Island—a volcanic cone formed after Mount Mazama collapsed and created the caldera that holds the lake and the island.

Below: Artist Jaime Quitero's rendering of Crater Lake on a clear, summer afternoon. The four block diagrams show the stages of volcanism leading to Mount Mazama's collapse:
1) Magma spews forth from the earth's interior a half million years ago as the cone-building stage begins.
2) Vents and cones develop on the mass, weakening it.
3) About 4850 BC, the mountain loses internal support and collapses when the mass blew out of the cone.
4) The explosion created the caldera which Crater Lake now occupies.

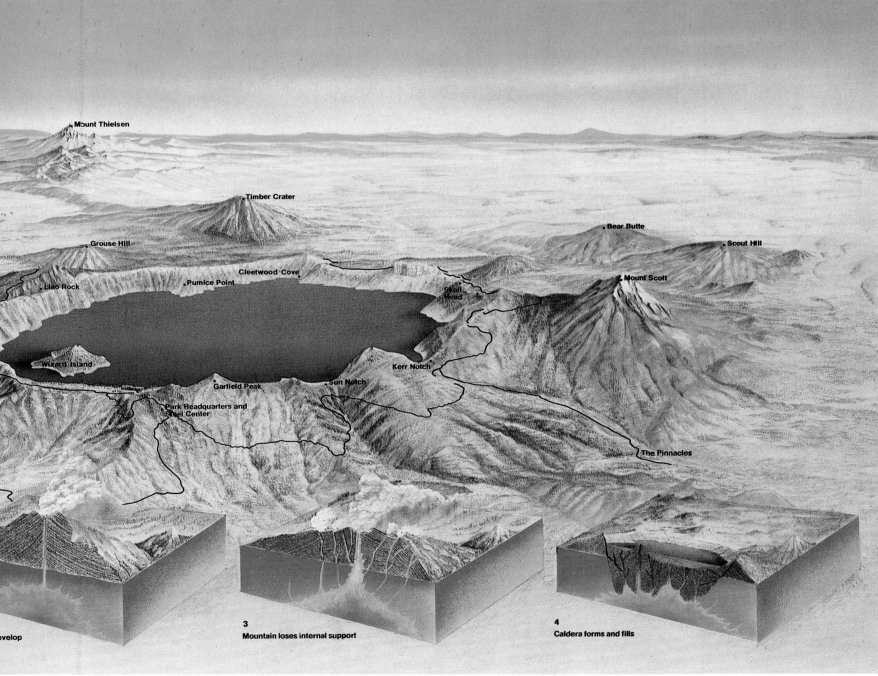

These pages: *In addition to simply enjoying the lake's scenic beauty, park visitors can have fun cross country skiing or snowmobiling.*

Great Basin, Nevada

Established: 1986   Acreage: 76,800

In an area of wide basins and high mountain ranges lies Great Basin National Park, the newest park in the United States. The park includes the former Lehman Caves National Monument and Wheeler Peak Scenic Area.

A highlight of the park is Lehman Caves, one of the largest limestone solution caverns found in the western United States. Over centuries, the chemical reaction between acid water and marble carved out the cave chambers. When the water table dropped below the cave floor, the cave was filled with air. As calcite-laden (the mineral from which marble is formed) water seeped down through the overlying rocks, it gathered as drops or spread out in thin films on the ceilings and sides of the cavern. As a result, hundreds of stalactites developed from the ceilings, growing longer and longer. In turn, water dripping from the stalactites built up stubby stalagmites.

The cave is also filled with other unusual rock formations. Thin, round disks of calcite are found in angular positions on the walls and floors of the cave. Pools of water have created beautifully terraced miniature dams around the edges. Huge, fluted columns reach from floor to ceiling. Twisting helictites—strange popcornlike lumps—grow on many of the formations themselves and cover walls and ceilings where the formations do not grow. They range in color from creamy white to orange to chocolate. Visitors to the park can take a tour through the varied color cave with its array of strange rock formations.

Wheeler Peak (13,063 feet/3982 meters), one of the highest mountains in the Great Basin, is the pinnacle of the impressive Snake Range, on the eastern edge of Nevada. An ascent of Wheeler Peak is an exhilarating alpine adventure, but only for those in good physical condition. Hiking trails lead to alpine lakes and a rare and ancient bristlecone pine forest. These trees are remarkable for their great age and their ability to survive adverse conditions. During harsh growing conditions, the living foliage dies back until the moisture and nutrients are sufficient for the remaining root system. A bristlecone pine found near Wheeler Peak was dated to be over 4900 years in 1964. Unfortunately, the tree was cut down before the area was protected as a national park.

The mountain slopes are covered with wildflowers and forests of aspen, pine, spruce, fir and mountain-mahogany. Mule deer feed in the mountain meadows, while, overhead, golden eagles soar.

Above right, top: Bristlecone pines, among the oldest trees in the world, are found in three groves in Great Basin National Park.

Above right, middle: Rising high above the floor of Lexington Canyon, this imposing natural arch was created by the forces of weather working slowly over a span of centuries.

Below: Upon reaching the summit of Wheeler's Peak, the mountain climber is rewarded with panoramic vistas of the Great Basin.

*The Parachute Shield (**above left**) and the Ivory Towers (**above**) in Lehman Caves are two unique rock formations delicately sculpted from deposits left by dripping water. Because there is no weather in the cave— no wind, no rain, no temperature changes—these formations will be preserved for tens of thousands of years.*

***Left:** Ranger-guided tours through Lehman Caves provide a fascinating view of this mysterious subterranean world.*

Haleakala, Hawaii

Established: 1960   Acreage: 28,655

Step into the contrasting beauty of Haleakala National Park—of cool and silent volcanic rocks, of cascading streams and quiet pools and of dazzling, silver plants and flashing, scarlet birds. Located on the island of Maui, Haleakala extends from the 10,023-foot summit of Mount Haleakala down the southeast flank to the Kipahulu coast near Hana. The park was created to preserve the outstanding features of Haleakala Crater, which is now a cool, cone-studded reminder of a once-active volcano. Streaks of red, yellow, gray and black trace the courses of recent and ancient lava, ash and cinder flows.

Maui, one of the younger islands in a chain of volcanic islands, began as two separate volcanoes on the ocean floor. Time and again the volcanoes erupted, spreading new layers of lava upon the old, until the two volcanoes were finally joined by a valley of ash. Haleakala, the larger, eastern volcano, reached a height of 12,000 feet (3600 meters) above the ocean. For awhile, volcanic activity ceased and the forces of wind and water shaped the island, cutting channels down the mountain slopes. When volcanic activity resumed, lava spewed down the stream valleys. Cones were formed from the cinders, ash and lava that were blown from numerous vents in the crater. The volcanoes of Maui have been quiet for several hundred years, but earthquake records indicate that internal adjustments are still taking place in the earth's crust. However, there is no sign of any volcanic activity today.

In contrast to the lava ash and cinder cones of Haleakala Crater are the lush greenness and abundant water of the Kipahulu section of the park. Here the visitor is greeted by a chain of usually placid, sparkling pools, each connected by a waterfall or cascade. Oheo, the stream joining the pools, has many moods, and at times becomes a thundering torrent of whitewater burying these quiet pools as it churns and plunges headlong toward the ocean.

A pastoral scene of rolling grasslands and forested valleys surrounds the pools. Gingers and ti form an understory in forests of kukui, mango, guava and bamboo, while beach naupaka, false kamani and pandanus abound along the rugged coastal cliffs.

In the higher elevations a vast, native koa and ohi'a rain forest thrives, still fairly untouched by man. It is here that the endangered Maui nukupu'u, Maui parrotbill and other native birds still survive in a delicately balanced environment.

Right: A late afternoon trek to the summit of Mount Haleakala ends in a spectacular sunset, as the sun slowly disappears below the horizon.

Below: As the lava poured down the mountainside, it destroyed all living things, leaving a trail of rocks in its wake. Today, this stark but beautiful landscape testifies to the sheer force of those ancient volcanic eruptions.

Left: The incredible view from the crater rim seems to go on for miles and miles. The clouds roll in about midday, and—if only white billowing puffs—add to the majesty of the scene before you. Sometimes, however, the cloud cover is so dense that it obscures the view entirely.

Below: The floor of the Haleakala crater is dotted with pink and gray cinder cones.

***These pages:** Though dormant now, Haleakala was once a fiery river of molten lava. Could Haleakala erupt again? No one knows.*

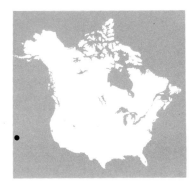

Hawaii Volcanoes, Hawaii

Established: 1916   Acreage: 299,177

The largest island in the Hawaiian archipelago, Hawaii is also one of earth's most extraordinary volcanic constructions. The ocean floor lies more than 18,000 feet below its beaches; the highest point on Mauna Kea is 13,796 feet above sea level; and Mauna Loa is 13,667 feet high. Measured from the ocean floor, these shield volcanoes are considered to be the greatest mountain masses on earth. It took Mauna Loa about three million years to attain its size: two million to reach the surface of the ocean and another million to form the vast mountain seen above sea level. Although Mauna Loa seems much bigger, Kilauea is also an impressive shield volcano, rising

Right: A curtain of fire rises boldly from Kilauea's east rift zone—the area of most recent activity.

Below: A lava river on Mauna Loa. When conditions are safe, park visitors can see for themselves the awesome spectacle of volcanic eruptions.

about 22,000 feet above the ocean floor; its height above sea level is slightly more than 4000 feet. Both are thought to be among earth's most active volcanoes.

Kilauea's activity is apparent almost everywhere within the bounds of the park. Its most recent displays have been along the east rift zone. Sometimes magma pushes its way through lateral conduits and flows from vents in a volcano's sides instead of in its summit crater—usually along the structural weaknesses in a shield volcano known as rift zones. Kilauea has two such zones.

Although they are active, Hawaii's volcanoes are gentle. Only twice in recorded history—in 1790 and 1924—have the volcanoes had violent outbursts characterized by explosions, clouds of poisonous gas, earthquakes, showers of mud and rains of erupted rock.

Hawaii Volcanoes also has a human history. Although the early Hawaiian people did not often venture near the summit of Kilauea, ruins of two religious heiau, or temples, have been reported near the caldera: one upon the bluff of Uwe-Kahuna, where the Hawaiian Volcano Observatory now stands; the other on Waldron Ledge, the high wall above Byron Ledge. At the southern end of the park, however, the ruins of several fishing villages lie among weeds. Adjoining the park museum at the Kalapana entrance are the remnants of one of ancient Hawaii's most sacred places, Waha'ula Heiau, the Temple of the Red-Mouthed God.

Despite their isolation from other islands and continents, Hawaii's volcanic mountains have an incredible diversity of plant and animal life. Seeds, spores, eggs and even living creatures were borne by the ocean currents, winds or birds to the islands. Over time, according to the laws of natural selection, new species evolved. Botanists believe that the 1700 species of Hawaiian plants evolved from fewer than 150 seeds or tiny plants. Unfortunately, when man arrived on the island he brought with him plants, animals and insects that destroyed, or contributed to the destruction of, many of Hawaii's plants.

Above: *Fountains and fumes from Pu'u'O'o on Kilauea's east rift zone.*

Right: *A channel of lava spews forth from the Pu'u'O'o vent on 2 June 1986.*

These pages: Fountains of fire along Mauna Loa's northeast rift. Compare this scene with the dormant crater of Haleakala on pages 184 to 185.

Lassen Volcanic, California

Established: 1916   Acreage: 106,372

Lassen Peak lies along the Ring of Fire, a chain of volcanoes—active, dormant and extinct—that circle the Pacific Ocean. This zone marks the edges of plates that compose the earth's crust. The movement of these plates creates volcanoes and earthquakes. As the expanding oceanic crust is thrust beneath the continental plate margins, it penetrates deep enough into the earth to be remelted. Pockets of molten rock result (magma), which become the feeding chambers for volcanoes.

About 500,000 years ago, Mount Tehama, a great Pacific Ring of Fire stratovolcano, gradually built up through countless eruptions. Lassen Peak began as a volcanic vent on Tehama's northern flank. It is considered the world's largest plug dome volcano, rising 2000 feet (610 meters) to attain the height of 10,457 feet (3200 meters) above sea level.

In May 1914, Lassen Peak erupted, beginning a seven-year

Right: The Devastated Area, with Lassen Peak looming in the background. Lassen Peak began as a volcanic vent on Mount Tehama's northern flank.

Below: Bumpass Hell, the largest geothermal area in the park, features fumaroles, boiling mud pots and waters above 212 degrees Fahrenheit. The man who named Bumpass Hell lost a leg as a result of falling into the boiling waters.

cycle of sporadic volcanic outbursts. The climax of this cycle occurred in 1915, when red lava spilled through a notch in the crater rim and flowed down the western slope a quarter of a mile, then hardened. On the northeast side the hot lava melted the deep snowfield, causing a huge river of mud to flow rapidly down the mountainside, carrying boulders the size of of an ordinary bedroom. Three days after that Lassen spewed an enormous mushroom cloud toward the sky. Meanwhile, on the northeast side another blast struck, widening the path of destruction to more than a mile, and continuing for five miles down the mountain, mowing down trees and all signs of life in its path. All of this activity generated nationwide attention, and brought about Lassen's establishemnt as a national park.

The Devastated Area and the Chaos Jumbles Area of the park demonstrate how landscapes recover from volcanic activity. Both are important post-volcanism plant succession sites that are recovering directly to conifers without preparation by herbaceous plants. Many disturbed areas throughout the park are reforested with young forests much more varied than the original forests. The reason for this appears to be the lack of competition during the early stages of growth. Eventually, only a portion of the trees now present will take control of the area. The park's plant life is a mix of species from the Sierra Nevada and the Cascades, which results in an abundance of species. Lassen boasts 715 plant species, while nearby Mount Shasta has only 485.

The Lassen area was a meeting point for four Indian groups who camped here on a seasonal basis. In 1911 a Yahi Indian named Ishi appeared in Oroville. Ishi's appearance was quite a surprise because his tribe was thought to be nonexistent. He lived out his days at the University of California Museum, where he was an invaluable ethnological resource. Ishi was considered the last Stone Age survivor in the United States.

`California's gold rush in 1848 brought the first white settlers. Two pioneer trails, developed by William Nobles and Peter Lassen, are associated with the park. In 1851 Nobles discovered an alternate route to the state, passing through Lassen. Sections of the Nobles Emigrant Trail are still visible in the park.

Above: *Kings Creek meanders through the Upper Meadow in the shadow of Lassen Peak (10457 feet/3187 meters).*

Right: *Eruptions also occurred in 1851 in the northeastern part of the peak at Cinder Cone, but the area has not recovered as quickly as the other sections of the park.*

Mount Rainier, Washington

Established: 1899   Acreage: 235,404

So overwhelming is the presence of Mount Rainier—it reaches 14,410 feet—that not much attention is paid to the park's encircling forest. On a clear day one can see the peak's snowfields from over 100 miles away. For those driving toward the park, one loses the great peak behind successively closer ranges. When finally the lower peaks are behind and the mountain looms directly ahead, nearly 8000 feet higher than anything nearby, one realizes it is a truly awe-inspiring mountain.

Mount Rainier is the fifth highest mountain on the United States, outside of Alaska. Mount Rainier has approximately 40 square miles of glacial rivers on its summit. The Emmons Glacier, about four and a quarter miles long and one mile wide, is the largest glacier in the lower 48 states. Carbon Glacier on the north face of the mountain is six miles long. Rainier's glacial system has steadily decreased in size over the past centuries, but is today recognized as the largest single peak glacial system in the 48 contiguous states. Rainier's glaciers total 41 in number.

Mount Rainier is a dormant volcano. The mountain used to be taller than it is today, but as eruptions diminished, the volcano began to deteriorate by explosion, collapse and erosion. The slopes of lava flows on opposite sides of the mountain project more than 100 feet above the present summit. The upper portion of the cone was probably removed by explosions and landslides. Liberty Cap and Point Success are remnants of the sides of the old higher cone. The current summit is Columbia Crest, at 14,410 feet, and lies on the rim of a small, recent lava cone.

Before the discovery of the area by explorers, Indian tribes lived in the lowlands surrounding the mountain. During the

summer they would move up the slopes to hunt and gather berries, bulbs and herbs. Mount Rainier was named by the British Captain George Vancouver during his exploration of the area in 1792, after his friend Admiral Peter Rainier. The first recorded climb to the summit was made by Hazard Stevens and Philimon Beecher Van Trump in 1870, who made the ascent from the south side of the mountain. Their Indian guide, Sluiskin, feared the mountain and begged them not to attempt the climb to the summit. He waited at their camp, and when the two climbers returned the next day, Sluiskin believed they were their ghosts returning to haunt him.

A variety of wildlife lives in the park, including bear, mountain goats, deer, elk, mountain lions, beavers, marmots, rabbits, and raccoons, as well as many smaller mammals—squirrels, chipmunks, mice, moles and shrews. Eagles occasionally soar overhead, dippers dive in the streams, and thrushes can be heard whistling in the deep forests. Other bird species include ptarmigan, stellar jays, gray jays, Clark's nutcrackers and ravens. The forests surrounding the mountains are composed of Douglas fir, hemlock, cedar and several species of fir. Ferns, mosses, lichen and a variety of fungi grow in the lowlands.

Below: The forests surrounding Mount Rainier bestow a feeling of serenity on the park visitor.

Left: Black bear can sometimes be seen ambling through Mount Rainier National Park.

Below: Conveying an overwhelming sense of power and majesty, Mount Rainier reigns supreme over the lower mountain ranges.

North Cascades, Washington

Established: 1968   Acreage: 505,000

This wildly mountainous region, according to Henry Custer, an American topographer surveying the international boundary in 1859, 'must been seen, it cannot be described.' The area which he tried to describe is now the North Cascades National Park Service Complex, composed of the North Cascades National Park and Ross Lake and the Lake Chelan National Recreation Areas. The complex sits deep in the wild, nearly impenetrable, northernmost reaches of the Cascade Range in northwest Washington.

The North Cascades—the mountains and all they imply— are the primary attraction. They are the culmination of the great Cascade Range that runs from northern California's volcanic Lassen Peak all the way into Canada. South of the range is a vast, high plateau whose profile is only periodically punctuated by jutting, isolated volcanic peaks. But in the park complex, an unbridled chaos of alpine peaks juts skyward in close formation. The park encompasses 318 glaciers—more than half of all the glaciers in the lower 48 states. There are few roads into the park, but from the park's many trails spectacular views unfold of glacially sculpted valleys and fields of ice and snow. The high mountain passes reveal panoramas of flower-sprinkled hillsides and meadows, rock ridges and cascading waterfalls. The animal most often seen by hikers is the mule deer. It migrates to the high meadows in the summer, returning to the lowland valleys in the winter.

Below: A high country stream edged by a dense forest is just a small part of the stunning mountain scenery of North Cascades National Park.

Rarely seen is the mountain cougar, a retiring animal and a hunter of small mammals, birds and deer.

Canadian fur trader Alexander Ross was the first European known to have crossed the Cascade crest, via the Twisp River and Copper Pass in 1814, in search of beaver and sites to promote the Northwest Company's fur trapping business. His last Indian guide, fearing supernatural reprisal for having trespassed on the realm of the gods, finally deserted Ross because of a fierce storm that struck after they reached the Skagit River. The handful of explorers who followed Ross also commented on the region's rugged, isolated nature. From 1880 to 1910, miners prospected for gold, lead, zinc and platinum. Although moderate strikes were recorded, transportation was arduous and profits limited, so mining was abandoned. About the turn of the century a few people tried their hands at logging and homesteading. Establishment of this area as a national park was bitterly contested by the lumber industry. Today, however, this land of jagged, jumbled, snow-capped mountains lures the backpacker, mountain climber, foothills walker and ardent scenery gazer.

Right: Heather Meadows abloom with wildflowers. In the distance lies snow-capped Mount Shuksan.

Below: Whatcom Peak (7575 feet/2309 meters) and Challenger Glacier. More than half of all the glaciers in the continental United States are in North Cascades National Park.

These pages: *Shrouded in thick clouds, the steep, dark peaks of the North Cascades reach high into the heavens.*

Olympic, Washington

Established: 1946   Acreage: 914,579

Olympic National Park has often been referred to as three great parks rolled into one because of its scenic ocean strip, lush, temperate rain forest and great mountainous core.

Some 57 miles of Pacific Ocean coastline form a vital component of the park. Unchanged except for the impact of the pounding surf and the mainland storms, the coastline looks much the same as it did when early Indians built their villages thousands of years ago. Drift logs cast high on the beach; sculptured arches and sea stacks; the roar of crashing waves; the calls of gulls, bald eagles and black oyster-catchers—all impress themselves upon the visitor.

It is the temperate rain forest for which the park has been internationally recognized as a Biosphere Reserve and World Heritage Site. Such rain forests are rare. They can be found only in New Zealand, southern Chile and on the northwest coast of the US. Necessary to these forests are a mild coastal climate, which rarely freezes in winter or goes above 80 degrees Fahrenheit in summer, about 12 feet of rain a year and some summer fog. The tree most closely associated with temperate rain forests in North America is the Sitka spruce. In addition to the Sitka spruce, temperate rain forests are characterized by nurse logs, which are fallen Sitka spruce upon which seedlings grow; colonnades, the trees standing in a row as a result of starting on nurse logs; trees standing on stilts; a profusion of mosses and lichens; and big leaf maples with clubmoss draperies.

A temperate rain forest is inhabited by a population of animals including black tailed deer, cougar, black bear, river otter, Douglas squirrel, jumping mouse and shrew. The park is famous for its huge Olympic, or Roosevelt elk, a species that can weigh up to 1000 pounds. Birds, such as the varied thrush, western robin, winter wren, pileated woodpecker, gray jay and raven, add texture to the fabric of the temperate rain forest.

The Olympic Mountains are not very high—Mount Olympus, the highest, is just under 8000 feet—but they rise almost from the water's edge. About 35 million years ago disturbances deep within the earth created huge underwater mountains. Eventually, some of the mountains were forced upward to the surface of the ocean to become the forerunners of today's Olympic Mountains. Powerful forces fractured, folded and overturned rock formations, creating the jumbled appearance of the Olympics. Later, streams and glaciers carved peaks and valleys, creating the beautiful and craggy landscape. Because the mountains are located on a peninsula, geographic isolation has given rise to several unique species of plants and animals. The most striking example is the Olympic marmot, with its distinctive chromosomal and behavioral patterns.

Far right: Temperate rain forest, one of the hallmarks of Olympic National Park. Notice the fallen logs, where seedlings take root. As the seedlings grow, they send their roots down the log into the ground. Eventually, the log rots away completely, leaving a row of young trees on stiltlike roots.

Below: *Point of Arches, on the wild and rocky Pacific Ocean coastline.*

Above: *Though only a short distance from the coast, the mountains of Olympic National Park seem a world away.*

Right: *The tidepools—isolated pockets of water among the rocks—are filled with a vast array of marine creatures that must adapt to a constantly changing environment. At low tide, they face the drying rays of the sun. At high tide, they confront the pounding surf. To deal with these changes, nature has equipped limpets with flattened shells that reduce the impact of the crushing waves. Snails seal themselves with small trap doors to prevent moisture loss, while anemones cover their soft bodies with broken shells.*

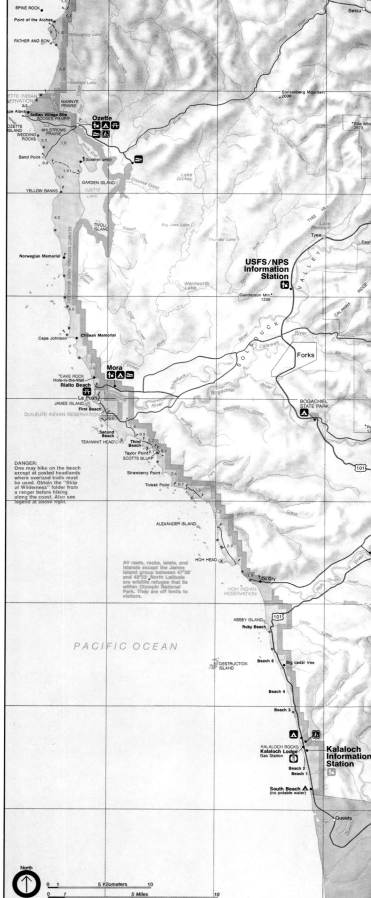

Above: *The Hoh Rain Forest. Almost every bit of space is taken up with a living plant, and, in fact, some plants even live on others. These are the epiphtyes—plants that do not come into contact with the earth.*

Right: *The bald eagle can sometimes by seen soaring in the skies above the park. They build their nests on inaccessible cliff ledges or high in tall trees.*

Left: *Cougars dwell in the temperate rain forests of Olympic National Park.*

Right: *Coastal strip near Kalaloch. Digging for razor clams, smelting with dip nets and surf fishing are popular activities at Kalaloch.*

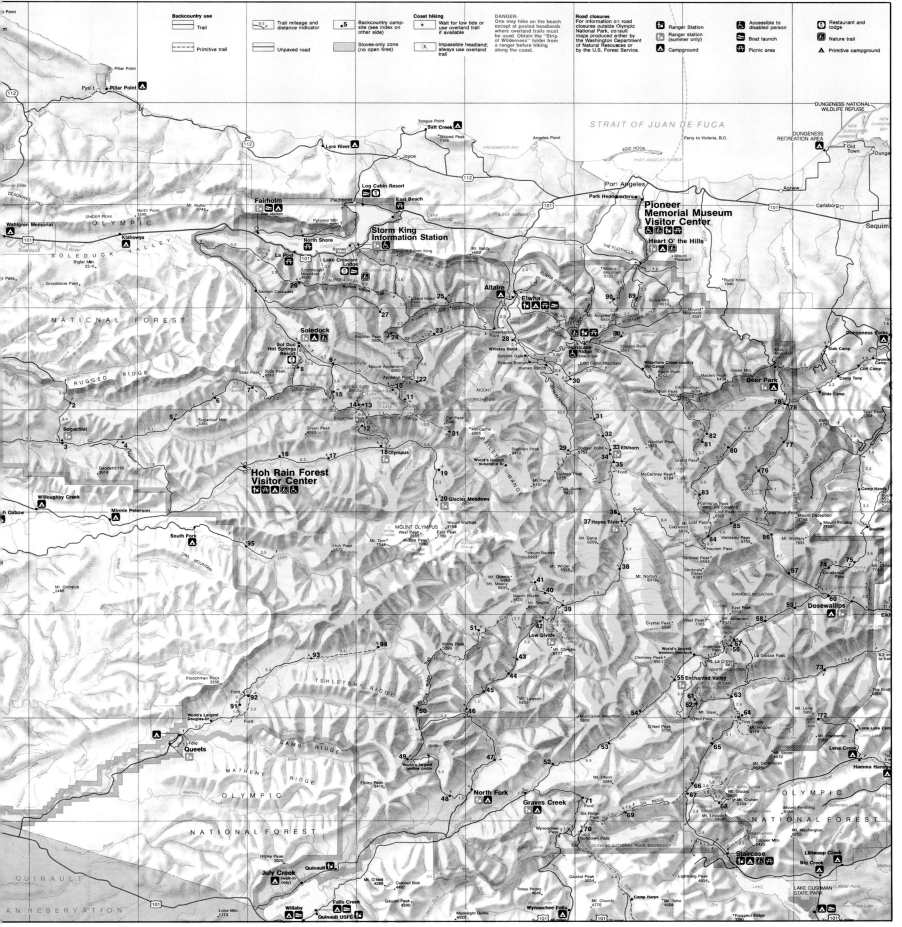

Pacific Rim, British Columbia

Established: 1970   Acreage: 96,000

The Pacific Ocean, named for its peaceful appearance the day that the Spanish explorer Balboa set eyes on it in 1513, not only gives this national park its name but is one of the major reasons for its existence. The park is located on Vancouver Island, beginning at the deep-sea port of Port Alberni, and is divided into three units: Long Beach, the Broken Group Island, and the West Coast Trail—each of which is separated from the others by expanses of land and water.

The historic 48 mile (77 kilometer) West Coast Trail once served shipwrecked sailors whose ships were battered by the heavy seas and high winds along this coastline, later known as the 'Graveyard of the Pacific.' After a large 1906 wreck, the federal government began construction of a lighthouse at Pachena Point and a lifesaving trail connecting lighthouses at Cape Beale and Carmanah Point with other lighthouses and towns toward Victoria. The intention was to build a trail between Bamfield and Carmanah Point (29 miles, 47 kilometers) so that shipwrecked sailors could easily reach coastal communities. Today, hiking the West Coast Trail, which covers deep gullies and steep slopes, takes between six and eight days to traverse and demands stamina and expertise in camping and hiking skills.

The Long Beach unit was named for the seven-mile (11

kilometer) stretch of surf swept sand and rocky headlands. The area is accessible by car from Port Aberni along a winding mountain highway, but the beach itself is not open to vehicle traffic. Hiking is the best way to enjoy the beaches, headlands and forests of the Long Beach unit. Many of the trails lead the hiker through the wooded areas of the park. Within Pacific Rim, there are six different forest communities: spruce fringe, cedar-hemlock forests, climax rain forests, wooded bogs, stream banks and roadsides, and forestry plantations. Camping and fishing are other popular activities.

Access to the Broken Group Islands is by boat across open ocean channels whose waves and reefs are at times hazardous. Boating conditions are good in the protected waterways of the inner islands. However, the waters are filled with reefs and are often obscured by heavy morning fog.

Because the park is on the Pacific flyway, thousands of migrating geese, ducks and shore birds pause to feed and rest on the beaches and estuaries in spring and fall. Pileated woodpecker, Stellar's jay, brown creeper, red crossbill and chestnut-backed chickadee dwell in the forests. Along the shore, one can spot various sandpipers and gulls, the great blue heron, bald eagle and black oystercatcher. Diving ducks, grebes, cormorants, loons, gulls and mures frequent the waters of the park. The rocky shoreline, with its tidal pools, sea caves and surf-swept headlands supports a variety of marine life—hermit crabs, limpets, seaweed, mussels and barnacles. Each spring gray whales pass close by the shore in their annual northward migration. Some of the whales stay along the coast all summer, and a few will even stay year round.

Below: Glistening sand and clear blue waters lure hikers, sunbathers and campers to Schooner Cove on Long Beach.

Above: For thousands of years, spring along the west coast of Vancouver has been heralded by the annual northern migration of gray whales.

Right: The eared grebe is one of the over 250 species of birds that have been spotted in Pacific Rim National Park.

Redwood, California

Established: 1968   Acreage: 110,131

The coast redwood towers over all other trees in the world. At 367.8 feet, the coast redwood discovered on the banks of Redwood Creek by the National Geographic Society in 1963 is the tallest known tree. Redwoods develop the greatest reported volume of living matter per unit of land surface. The giant sequoias, cousins to the coast redwoods, grow larger in diameter and bulk, but not as tall. The coast redwood live an average of 500 to 700 years, although some live to be 2000. The living tree has no known killing diseases, and insects cause it little harm. The redwood's worst enemy is fire, but

Right: *Playful river otters frolic in and around the creeks of Redwood National Park.*

Facing page and below: *A walk among the giant redwoods overwhelms the senses but quiets the emotions.*

sometimes a strong wind will topple it because it has such a shallow root system. Although coast redwoods require much rain, frequent summer fog seems to be the most important factor in their growth. The fog decreases the trees' loss of water through evaporation and transpiration and adds moisture to the soil.

Redwood forests have lived in the Northern Hemisphere since the time of the dinosaurs. Dramatic changes in geology and climate have reduced them to the present natural range. Redwood National Park stretches along California's North Coast from north of Eureka to just south of the Oregon border. The terrain here is so rough it is not surprising that it took Jedediah Smith, the first European to trek here overland, ten days just to cover the last few miles to the coast in 1828. This forbidding character helped protect magnificent coast redwood groves until gold fever 20 years later brought eventual settlement—and the need for wood products. Commercial logging lasted for over 100 years. Finally, in the 1960s, the rapid depletion of the redwood forests prompted concerned citizens to call for the preservation of these magnificent trees in local, state and national parks.

There is more to Redwood National Park than its spectacular trees. During spring and fall migration the park boasts 300 species of birds, of which roughly half are associated with water. Bald eagles, peregrine falcons, brown pelicans and the Aleutian Canada Goose are all endangered species protected under the park.

The most commonly seen mammal is the Roosevelt elk, but mountain lions and blacktail deer also live in the park. Off shore, marine mammals—particularly the gray whale—migrate. Porpoises, seals, sea lions and other whales can also be seen. The intertidal zone alone boasts 168 invertebrate species. Freshwater areas are populated by river otters, mink and beaver. Fifteen of the 22 species of salamander native to western North America are found here.

Sequoia, California

Established: 1890   Acreage: 418,623

Kings Canyon, California

Established: 1940   Acreage: 460,136

Sequoia and Kings Canyon National Parks are administered as a single unit. These two adjacent parks are the home of the giant sequoia. This massive tree escaped the last Ice Age and stands as a survivor of an ancient lineage of huge trees that mantled much of the earth millions of years ago. Today these trees grow only in scattered groves on the western slope of the Sierra Nevada, the mountains that the famous naturalist John Muir called 'the Range of Light.' In volume of total wood, the giant sequoia stands alone as the largest living thing on earth. One tree lives longer; one has a greater diameter. Three others grow taller. None is larger. The age of the General Sherman tree, the largest of the sequoias, is estimated at 2200 years. The estimated weight of the trunk is 1385 tons; height above the base, 274.9 feet; and circumference at the ground, 102.6 feet. The diameter of General Sherman's largest branch is over six and a half feet. Few records show mature sequoias ever having died from disease or insect attack. Instead, they usually die of toppling!

The parks are unique in that their comparatively small area embraces many peaks more than 14,000 feet above sea level. Mount Whitney in the Sequoia portion is the highest point (14,495 feet/4418 meters) in the continental United States. The two parks encompass a vast stretch of the Sierra crest and the slightly less high intermediate crest known as the Great Western Divide. Here, one can find fascinating cirques, serrated ridges and crests and abruptly changing valley gradients. The parks contain classic examples of hanging valleys, moraines and related geological features. There are also more than 1000 glacial lakes nestled high in the mountains. Sequoia and Kings Canyon National Parks encompass sweeping mountain grandeur and minute floral beauties. The high mountain peaks and deep canyons match the sheer majesty of

the giant sequoia. Hikers and backpackers can experience all of this from the parks' many trails.

White settlers first came to the Sierra Nevadas around 1850. They encountered two tribes of Indians—the Western Mono in the upper foothills and the Yokuts in the lower foothills—already there, hunting game, gathering fruit and living in peace with one another. The white men first looked for gold, but soon ranches started. Over the next twenty years, men sought new ways to use the area's resources, and sawmills began to appear. The rapid destruction of the Sierran forest threatened to destroy the mountain watersheds needed for the farms in the San Joaquin Valley. Consequently, a campaign to preserve the forests was successfully mounted, and in 1890 Congress established Sequoia and General Grant National Parks. Other lands were subsequently protected, and in 1940 Kings Canyon National Park was created from the new lands and General Grant National Park.

Previous pages: Deep blue Eagle Lake rests high in the sublime Sierra Nevada mountains of Sequoia National Park.

Above right: General Sherman—the world's largest tree—is nearly 275 feet (84 meters) tall and has a base circumference of over 102 feet (32 meters).

Right: Mount Whitney, from Timberline Lake. At 14,495 feet (4418 meters), Mount Whitney is the highest point in the continental United States.

Facing page: Grand Sentinel (8504 feet/2592 meters) stands guard over Zumwalt Meadow.

South Moresby/ Gwaii Haanas, British Columbia

Established: 1988   Acreage: 363,330

Located off the coast of British Columbia in the Queen Charlotte Islands, Canada's newest park reserve encompasses 138 islands and 1000 miles (1600 km) of coastline, an area known as the Canadian Galapagos. A wilderness park of beautiful and unique landscapes, the area is brimming with life, both on land and in the sea. Wildlife includes 25 percent of British Columbia's nesting seabirds and 11 species of whales. The black bear found on the islands is believed by some scientists to be the world's largest black bear. Considered a separate subspecies, the island black bear has a larger skull and different tooth formation than the mainland species. The primeval rainforests and lush alpine meadows are inhabited by plants and animals not found anywhere else in the world. At least 14 species of flowering plants are unique to the Queen Charlotte Islands. The islands are considered to be biologically significant because of the great range in numbers of plants and animals, as well as species diversity. It is likely that the islands were a refuge during the last Ice Age. In recent years, mainland species, such as black-tail deer, beaver and racoon, were introduced to the islands—an action that has prompted some concern among environmentalists because the new species are having a profound effect on the native plants and animals.

Access to the park is by boat or aircraft; both water and air access are very expensive, and there is no fuel available in the park reserve. The park reserve is remote from the nearest road (25 miles/40 kilometers). Facilities are limited so that the primitive and wilderness qualities of the area will be preserved. The area has been visited and sporadically populated by non-native people for only about the last 150 years.

Today, the park reserve is essentially unpopulated, with the exception of of two small enclaves. The Haida people continue to use the land and sea resources of the archipelago, as they have for centuries. 'Gwaii Haanas' is the Haida name for the area, meaning place of wonder. This fragile land includes a rich legacy of Haida culture, as exemplified at Ninstints, a World Heritage Site. Located on Anthony Island, Ninstints is a remarkable example of an Old Haida village site, with free-standing totems and longhouse remains.

Below: South Moresby remains a wild, isolated land. A visit to the park is a step back in time— to an unspoiled land uninhabited by man.

Left: This remote and beautiful land off the coast of British Columbia is accessible only by boat or air.

Below: The totem poles at Ninstints—an old Haida village. Time has had little effect on the Haida people; they continue to live much as they did centuries ago.

211

These pages: *A lone kayaker plies the waters of Windy Bay at Lyell Island, South Moresby/ Gwaii Haanas.*

Yosemite, California

Established: 1890   Acreage: 760,917

Yosemite, whose natural wonders have been praised by writers, artists and photographers ever since gold was discovered in the Sierra Nevada foothills in 1849, is one of the best known national parks in the world. As its fame spread throughout the world, hotels and houses were built, livestock grazed in the meadows, orchards were planted and abuse of the land prevailed. Spurred by the specter of private exploitation of this splendor, a few conservationists took action. John Muir's struggle against devastation of the High Sierra meadows resulted in the federal legislation that created the park.

Tuolumne Meadows and the high country has some of the most rugged, yet sublime, scenery in the Sierra. The meadows put on a spectacular show of color in the early summer as the wildflowers bloom. Tuolumne Meadows, at 8600 feet, is the largest subalpine meadow in the Sierra. It has long been a popular starting point for summer backpacking trips and day hikes and is growing in popularity as a winter mountaineering area.

Mariposa Grove is the largest of three sequoia groves in the park. The Grizzly Giant in the Mariposa Grove is 2700 years old and is considered the oldest of all sequoias. Amazingly, these tall giants have existed since the beginning of history of the western world and have endured in spite of man's interference. In the late 1800s, tunnels were cut through two trees in the Mariposa Grove. Sometimes even the best intentions of man created problems for the sequoia. Man's desire to protect the sequoia from fire interfered with its ability to reproduce.

Far right: A spectral moon hangs in the heavens above Half Dome in Yosemite Valley.

Facing page: Yosemite Falls roars to the floor of the Valley. This extraordinary waterfall is among the highest in the world.

Below: Like the writers, artists and photographers who were drawn to the Yosemite Valley over a hundred years, people still come here to revel in the land's incomparable beauty.

Frequent natural fires are needed to open the seeedbed and thin out competing species. The National Park Service now has prescribed burnings to stimulate this vital process, and young sequoia are more abundant.

Yosemite Valley, 'The Incomparable Valley,' is most likely the world's best known example of a glacier-carved canyon. Its leaping waterfalls, towering cliffs, rounded domes and massive monoliths make it a preeminent natural wonder. The valley is characterized by sheer walls and a flat floor. When alpine glaciers moved through the canyon of Merced River, the ice carved through weaker sections of granite, plucking and scouring rock but leaving harder, more solid portions—such as El Capitan and Cathedral Rocks—intact. When the glacier melted, it created ancient Lake Yosemite. The lake was eventually filled in by sediment, forming the flat valley floor. The same process is now at work on Mirror Lake. The valley teems with life, from open meadows of wildflowers and flowering shrubs to forests of ponderosa pine, cedar and Douglas fir, from monarch butterflies to mule deer to black bear.

The vista from Glacier Point is so vast—and spectacular—that it overwhelms the viewer. From this vantage point, one can see the length and breadth of the valley and the entire drop of Yosemite Falls. And beyond it all—in breathtaking clarity—lies the High Sierra.

Indians had lived in Yosemite Valley and surrounding areas for centuries before the white man came. In 1851 soldiers, the Mariposa Batallion, were dispatched there by the governor of California. Within a decade the valley was established as a tourist attraction. Some sections of the population soon realized that something must be done to govern the land's use to protect its ecology. Congress enacted a law, and on 30 June 1864, President Lincoln signed it, granting Yosemite Valley and the Mariposa Grove of Giant Sequoias to California to be held 'inalienable for all time.' Thus Yosemite became the first state park in the United States.

Far left: El Capitan, as seen from the Merced River. At every turn, one beholds amazingly beautiful sights.

Below: Cliffs near Tioga Pass. These sheer walls challenge as well as delight the experienced mountain climber.

Right: Vernal Falls, with a height of 317 feet (97 meters), is one of the many waterfalls that circle Yosemite Valley.

Far right: Regal Half Dome, formed when glaciers chipped away layers of rock from the more solid granite, rises high above Yosemite Valley.

Below: Hikers bask in the wondrous view from Glacier Point. In the distance are Vernal Falls and Nevada Falls.

THE
FAR NORTH

Many of the Far North's parks are in Alaska, a land that warrants an introduction, for it is expansive as well as diverse. In climate and topography, 'the Great Land' constitutes a virtual subcontinent. The Alaskan waters, from the deep bays to the dramatic fiords, are home to whales, seals, sea otters and many other sea mammals. The mountains feature glaciers, volcanoes and the tallest peaks in the United States.

Reports by early explorers and naturalists tell of the vast Arctic lands teeming with herds of caribou, the seemingly uninhabitable terrain that was the ancestral home of cultures dating back to the end of the Ice Age, and winters of deadening cold giving way to balmy summers that warm vast nurseries for migratory birds destined for every state and all continents of the world.

The Alaska Lands Act (1980) created or expanded eight national parks and established two national monuments and 10 national preserves. The National Park System in Alaska now contains more than 51 million acres, or 13 percent of the state's 375 million acres. These lands and waterways make up the finest natural and cultural resources remaining in public ownership—an enduring frontier.

free in summer and supports an extensive tundra of lichen, moss heath and a few dwarf shrubs. Dominating the highlands is the Penny Ice Cap, which covers 3540 square miles (5698 square kilometers), making it one of the largest icecaps in the northern hemisphere. A rolling, hilly landscape filled with boulders and moraine surrounds the highlands. The boulders are covered with lichen, and in the summer the rocky slopes are hidden by a cover of flowering plants. Scattered icefields lie high in the uplands.

The fiords are inhabited by whales, narwhals, seals and walruses. On land, Arctic fox and caribou make their home. Many endangered species—polar bear, Atlantic walrus, and blue, humpback and right whales—are found in the area. Roughly 40 species of birds, including Canada goose, snowy owl and the rare whistling swan, nest in the park.

Baffin Island was a site of the Thule culture a thousand years ago. Archaeologists have discovered the ruins of several Thule communities near Cumberland Sound. Today there are two Inuit settlements near the park, one at Pangnirtung and the other on Broughton Island. As with all the national parks in the far north, the traditional lifestyle of the native population is respected, and the northern natives continue to fish and hunt in the park.

Auyuittuq, Northwest Territories

Established: 1972   Acreage: 5,305,600

Auyuittuq National Park, on the Cumberland Peninsula of Baffin Island, represents the vast arctic regions that make up more than one-third of Canada's landscape. Lying along the sixtieth parallel, the park contains spectacular fjords and deeply carved mountains dominated by a huge icecap.

Auquittuq's Arctic coastline is cut into by roughly graded valleys and fjords as long as 29 miles (48 km), with steep cliffs rising above the sea. Mountains are crossed by long, narrow valleys, many of which are filled with glaciers. The 60-mile (97 kilometer) Pangnirtung Pass is essentially ice-

Below: *Almost all park visitors come to hike the Pangnirtung Pass—a rugged trip but the grandeur and isolation of the pass make it an unforgettable experience.*

Denali, Alaska

Established: 1980   Acreage: 6,000,000

Denali, or the 'High One,' is what the nearby Athabascan native peoples called the massive peak for which the park is named. As a result of the 1980 Alaska National Interest Lands Conservation Act, the boundary of former Mount McKinley National Park was enlarged and redesignated. Now slightly larger than Massachusetts, the park exemplifies interior Alaska's character as one of the world's last great frontiers offering an opportunity for wilderness adventure.

Mount McKinley is often considered Alaska's most impressive feature: It is the highest mountain on the North American continent. Measured from the 2000-foot lowlands

Right: A ptarmigan dressed in its winter finery. The ptarmigan and the gray jay (see page 226) are among the few species that winter in Denali.

Below: Grizzlies are adept at catching fish and will even fight for the best fishing spots.

near Wonder Lake to its summit, this mountain could be called the tallest in the world. The vertical relief of 18,000 feet, greater than that of Mount Everest, tops out on the summit at 20,320 feet. Mount McKinley reigns in lofty isolation over the Alaska range, that 600-mile arc of mountains that divides south-central Alaska from the interior plateau. Although not a difficult climb from a technical standpoint, the fierce winds and low temperatures combine to make the environment one of the harshest on earth. The north peak, at 19,740 feet (5934 meters), was first reached in 1910 by four Alaskans, but the south peak—the actual summit— was not conquered until Archdeacon Hudson Stuck, Walter Harper, Robert G Tatum and Harry Karstens made their attempt in 1913.

Native Athabascans traversed this area long before Caucasians found it. From spring through fall, they gathered fruits and edible plants and hunted for caribou, sheep and moose on the lowland hills of Denali's northern reaches. When the cold weather arrived, they headed to the river valleys at the lower elevations. Some tribes believed the mountain possessed supernatural powers and they may have altered their travel routes because of its perceived power over them.

Wildlife abounds in this harsh, northern environment. Dall sheep graze the alpine tundra and grizzly bear roam throughout the park. Moose, caribou and wolves as well as a number of smaller mammals also inhabit the park. Birdlife is interesting and varied, with over 157 species recorded. Golden eagles soar above the ridgetops, while the hawk owl, spruce grouse and varied thrush live in the forests. Raven, ptarmigan and gray jay are a few of the species that winter in Denali.

This expansive landscape, filled with grizzly bear and other large mammals, lies adorned with tiny plants. Only plants adapted to bitter cold weather can survive here, but Denali boasts over 430 species of flowering plants, mosses and lichens. The miniaturized beauty of the tundra plants and the wanderings of the young rivers provide a striking contrast to the lofty, isolated and often cloud-hidden grandeur of Mount McKinley.

Above: Mount McKinley looms tall and impressive as US Air Force jets thunder by.

Left: A young moose forages for food in the vast expanses of Denali National Park.

Right: The gray jay flies through the forests of the far north like a ghost.

Below: On a cold wintry day, the red fox will curl up in the snow, wrapping its tail around its nose and footpads for protection.

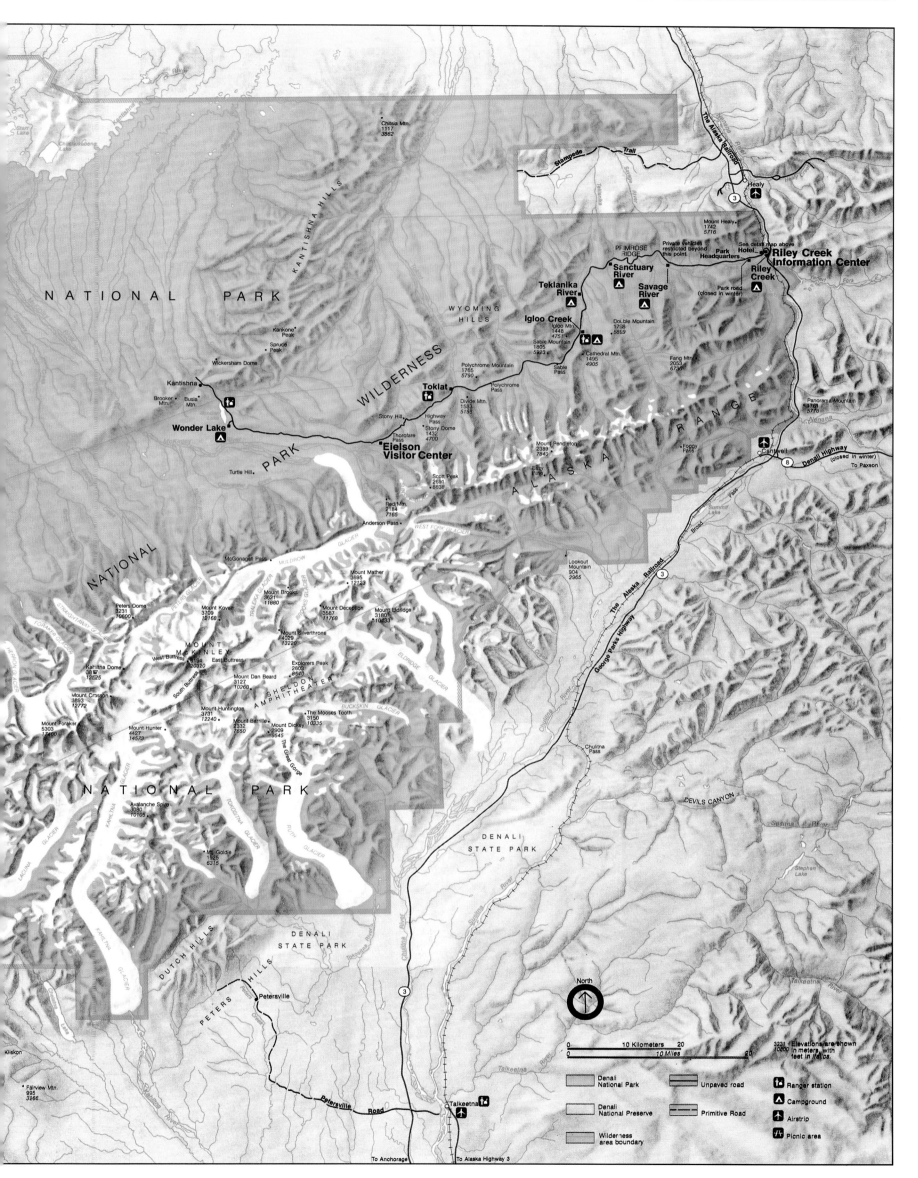

North

Denali
National Park

Denali
National Preserve

Wilderness
area boundary

Unpaved road

Primitive Road

Ranger station

Campground

Airstrip

Picnic area

3231 Elevations are shown
10600 in meters, with
feet in italics.

10 Kilometers 20

10 Miles 20

Ellesmere Island, Northwest Territories

Established: 1986   Acreage: 9,763,764

Located in the northernmost part of Canada, Ellesmere Island National Park Reserve includes mountain ranges, glaciers, fjords and Lake Hazen, the largest lake north of the Arctic Circle. The park is dominated by ice. Hundreds of glaciers, some that reach into the valleys and fiords, cover the area. Massive ice fields stretch across the park, while 'ice shelves' cling to the northern coast. High above the ice, Mount Barbeau, the highest of the Grant Land Mountains and the highest mountain in eastern North America, rises majestically. South of Mount Barbeau lies Lake Hazen and the Hazen Plateau, an upland area dissected by rivers, with tall cliffs overlooking Lady Franklin Bay.

The long, harsh winters and brief, cool summers and very low precipitation create a polar desert — a windswept and arid land, with few plants and little animal life. Yet in this harsh land there exist areas of thermal oases, warm moist regions that support plant and animal life. The Lake Hazen area, for example, has large populations of Arctic hare, which often gather in the hundreds, and small herds of musk oxen and Peary caribou. A few wolves, Arctic foxes and polar bear can also be seen, and about 30 species of birds visit the area.

Through the remains of ancient cultures, historians have pieced together the story of a nomadic people who crossed Ellesmere Island 4000 years ago. The land was warmer then, and it is believed these hunters followed the musk oxen as they migrated north, on a route now called the Musk Ox Way.

The first Europeans reached Ellesmere Island around 1850, and in 1875 HMS *Alert and Discovery* established a base at Fort Conger from which to make sled journeys inland and across to Greenland. Remains of the buildings at Fort Conger can still be seen, perched on the rocky terrain. Today communities of Inuit live in Grise Fiord and Resolute Bay, where they continue their centuries old way of life — hunting, fishing and trapping.

Far right: The arctic fox is one of the few animals that live in this far northern land.

Below: Lake Hazen—the largest lake north of the arctic circle— is a thermal oasis in this land of ice and snow.

Above: *During the brief summers on Ellesmere, the sun bathes the land in continuous daylight. There are no nights to mark the passage of time. Time and land seem endless.*

Left: *Musk oxen once roamed the arctic region in great numbers, but today they are relatively rare.*

Gates of the Arctic, Alaska

Established: 1980   Acreage: 7,500,000

This vast, remote park was created to perpetuate the fragile beauty of the Alaskan wilderness. The natural forces of wind, water, temperature and glacial and tectonic action have sculpted a widely varied landscape in the northernmost Rocky Mountains. The southern foothills rise into rugged peaks reaching in excess of 7000 feet. At the Arctic Divide, the slopes merge into the tundra and stretch for miles to the

Arctic Ocean. Countless waterways, including six national wild rivers—the Alatna, John, Kobuk, Noatuk, North Fork Koyukuk and Tinayguk—race through the park.

Within the park's borders lies a major portion of the range and habitat of the western Arctic caribou herd. Grizzly and black bears, wolves, moose, Dall sheep and wolverine also inhabit the park. Although the park has a diversity of wildlife, the animals are widely scattered because much land is needed to support life. Local birds, as well as migrating species from across the globe, are also found within Gates of the Arctic.

Sparse black spruce forests dot the north face of the mountains and poorly drained lowlands, while boreal forests of white spruce, aspen and birch are found on the southern slopes. Clusters of dwarf and resin birch, alder and willow are found at the tree line. The alder and tussocks grow thick, often making hiking difficult. Plants and animals grow quickly during the short summer, but most activities cease with the coming of the long, harsh winter. Little snow falls in the dry interior region, but what does fall endures, covering the land and rivers in a blanket of white ice.

Gates of the Arctic is a remote wilderness. There are no visitor facilities in the park. All visitors must be self-sufficient, and survival skills are essential. The perpetuation of the land's wild and undeveloped character is the primary goal of the park. In addition to preserving the fish and wildlife and their habitats, the 1980 legislation that created Gates of the Arctic also protects the subsistence way of life of the northern peoples who live in or nearby the park.

Above right: The fierce and determined wolverine lives in the vast expanses of Gates of the Arctic National Park.

Right: Park lands protect the habitat for the western arctic caribou herd that has been so vital to the economy of the Alaskan natives.

Facing page: Dall sheep inhabit the steep cliffs and rocky ledges of the park, but they are rarely seen by park visitors.

Overleaf: The ultimate wilderness—a remote, unpopulated land in the northernmost Rocky Mountains.

Glacier Bay, Alaska

Established: 1980   Acreage: 3,225,198

The shorelines of Glacier Bay were completely covered by ice just 2000 years ago. Explorer Captain George Vancouver found Icy Strait choked with ice in 1794, and Glacier Bay was a barely indented glacier. That glacier was more than 4000 feet thick, up to 20 miles or more wide, and extended more than 100 miles to the St Elias Range of mountains. By 1879 naturalist John Muir found that the ice had retreated 48 miles up the bay. By 1916 the Grand Pacific Glacier headed Tarr Inlet, 65 miles from Glacier Bay's mouth. Such rapid retreat is known nowhere else.

Glaciers form because the snowfall in the high mountains exceeds snow-melt. The snowflakes first change to granular snow—round ice grains—but the accumulating weight soon presses it into solid ice. Eventually, gravity sets the ice mass flowing downslope, usually far less than four to seven feet per day. The point at which the rate of melt equals the rate of accumulation is the glacier's terminus or snout. If the glacier's snout reaches tidal waters, it is called a tidewater glacier. The park includes 16 tidewater glaciers; 12 actively break off into the bay. The Johns Hopkins Glacier breaks off such volumes of ice that it is rarely possible to approach its ice cliffs closer than about two miles. The glaciers seen in the park today are remnants of a general ice advance—the Little Ice Age, which began about 4000 years ago—and which reached its maximum extent around 1750, when general melting began.

The snowcapped Fairweather Range supplies ice to all glaciers on the peninsula separating Glacier Bay from the Gulf of Alaska. Mount Fairweather, the range's highest peak, stands at 15,320 feet. In Johns Hopkins Inlet, some peaks rise from sea level to 6520 feet within just four miles of shore. The great glaciers of the past carved these fjords, or drowned valleys, out of the mountains like great troughs.

As the glacier retreats, plants and animals return to the land, and the landscape is reborn. Plant recovery begins with a 'black crust,' a layer of algae that stabilizes the silt and retains the water. Then moss appears, followed by scouring rush and fireweed, dryas, alders and willows. In succession come spruce and hemlock forests. Each successive plant community creates new conditions that lead to its replacement by the new, more competitive plants. For example, the alder add nitrogen to the soil, which allows the spruce to take hold and eventually shade out the alder.

The patterns by which animals re-inhabit the land are not as neatly mapped as plant succession, for there are no pioneer animal species leading the way. Even the act of returning is more difficult. Unlike plants, which can hitch rides on the wind or water, mammals must walk or swim. Bears, river otters and mink can swim around ice. Once on the virgin land, the mammals must adjust to conditions. Mountain goats can live on high ridges the ice exposed, and harbor seals can give birth on densely packed icebergs.

In addition to the glaciers, the park waters boast two of the great whales, the minke and humpback, and one smaller, the orca. To see these large creatures in their natural habitat is indeed a thrilling experience. Scientists have only recently begun studying the Glacier Bay whales. Unfortunately, most of our past knowledge about whales has come from man's attempt to harvest them, not to save them from extinction.

Below: The snowy owl survives in the arctic by feeding on mice and lemmings, but will head south to warmer climates if food becomes scarce.

Right: Harbor seals have adjusted well to life on the glaciers of Glacier Bay National Park.

Below: Sunrise at Margerie Glacier in the Fairweather Mountains is a spectacle put on by nature, witnessed only by a few.

Above: A magnificent flier, the size and presence of the bald eagle command respect. This awesome bird of prey thrives on the fish of Glacier Bay.

Right: The Alaskan brown, or grizzly, bear. Some authorities consider them separate species; others regard the grizzly and the brown bear as one in the same.

Right: The horned grebe builds its nest in the water. Social birds, they sometimes raise their young in groups.

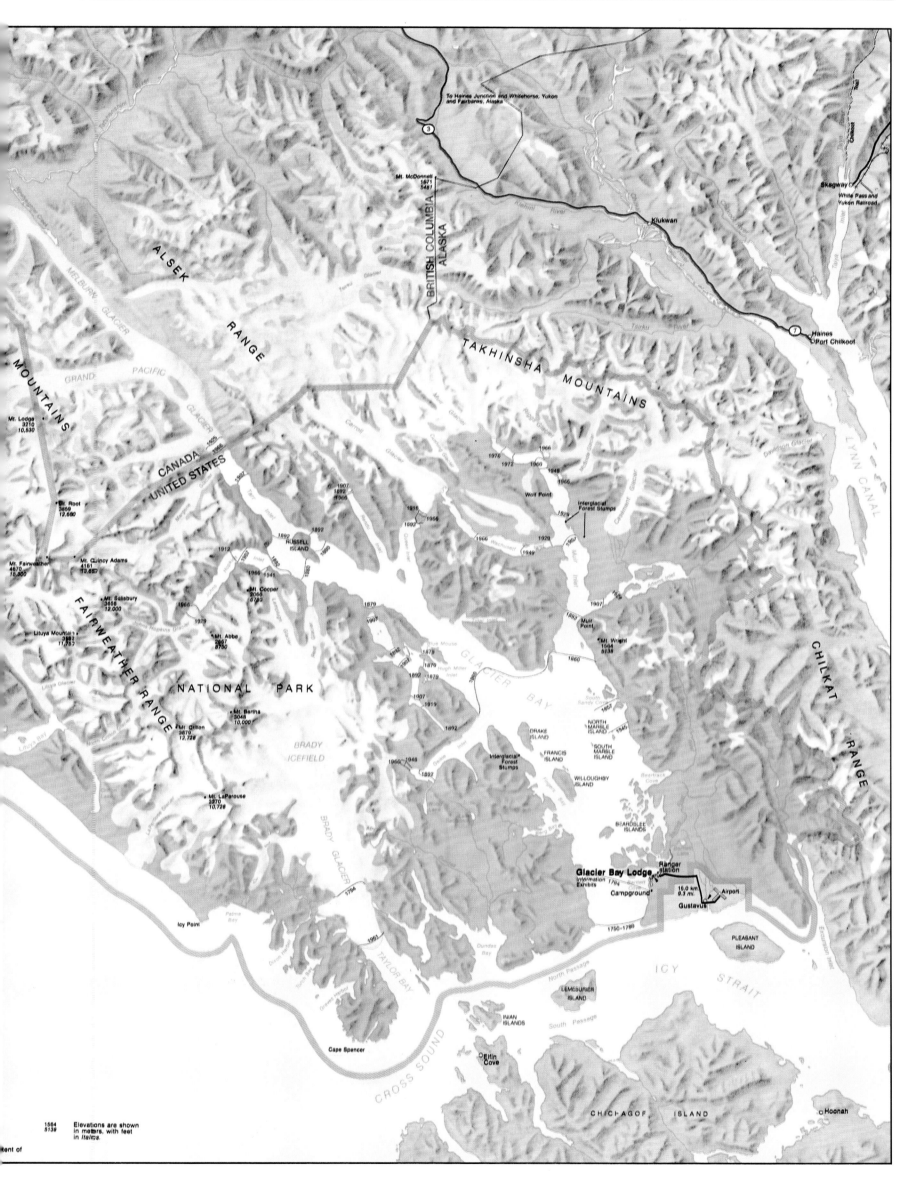

Katmai, Alaska

Established: 1980   Acreage: 3,716,000

Katmai was declared a national monument in 1918 to preserve the living laboratory of its cataclysmic volcanic eruption in June 1912. The blast was one of the most violent ever recorded. Great quantities of hot, glowing pumice and ash poured from Novarupta and flowed over the terrain, destroying everything in its path. More than 40 square miles (65 square kilometers) of once lush, green land lay covered with volcanic deposits 700 feet (200 meters) deep. Afterwards, in what would become known as the Valley of Ten Thousand Smokes, fumaroles by the thousands issued steam hot enough to melt zinc.

In exploring the area after the eruption, Robert Griggs found Mount Katmai's new crater lake and assumed Mount Katmai had erupted. The true source was actually the nearby Novarupta Volcano, although much of the erupted magma was drained from beneath Mount Katmai. The draining caused Mount Katmai's summit to subside, leaving a caldera in which the crater lake formed.

The intervening years have seen most of the geothermal features die out, but an equally compelling interest has arisen: to safeguard the area's huge brown bear—earth's largest terrestrial carnivore—which in summer fishes the park and preserve's streams to feast on migrating salmon. Mature male bears in Katmai may weigh up to 900 pounds. Mating occurs from May to mid-July, with the cubs born in dens in mid-winter. Up to four cubs may be born, at a mere one pound each. Cubs stay with the mother for two years, during which time she does not reproduce. Browns dig a new den each year, entering in November and emerging in April—about one-half of their lifetimes is spent in their dens.

In addition to the brown bear, Katmai is known for its salmon. The salmon run begins in late June. By the end of July a million fish have moved from Bristol Bay to the Naknek lakes and rivers. The salmon spawn during the next two months, and in the spring the young fish emerge from the gravel at the river bottom. They migrate to the larger lakes, where they will stay for about two years before moving on to the sea. After another two years, they will return to the place of their birth to spawn and begin the cycle all over again.

Katmai is so large and imposing that most of it is an unknown wilderness. The vast systems of elongated lakes nestle in valleys gouged out by glaciers. The lower slopes of interior mountains are covered with birch, poplar and spruce forests. In the alpine tundra of the higher slopes wildflowers abound in the short summer season. Deep bays, rock shoals, sheer cliffs and narrow beaches dot the rugged, indented coast.

Right: Katmai National Park is a land of volcanoes, rugged mountain peaks, enormous lakes and island-studded bays.

Below: Every year salmon burst from the Pacific Northwest and into the park waters to spawn.

Kenai Fjords, Alaska

Established: 1980   Acreage: 670,000

The Kenai Fjords are coastal mountain fjords whose placid seascapes reflect scenic icebound landscapes and whose salt spray mixes with mountain mist. The park features the seaward interface for the Harding Icefield, one of four major ice caps in the United States. Located on the southeastern Kenai Peninsula, the park is a pristine and rugged land supporting many unaltered natural environments and ecosystems.

Kenai Fjords National Park derives its name from the long, steep-sided, glacier-carved valleys that are now filled with ocean waters. The seaward ends of the Kenai Mountains are slipping into the sea, being dragged under by the collision of two tectonic plates of the earth's crust. What were once alpine valleys filled with glacier ice are now deepwater mountain-flanked fjords. The forces that caused this land to submerge are still present. In 1964, the Alaskan Good Friday earthquake dropped the shoreline six feet in just one day. As the land sinks into the ocean, glacier-carved cirques are turned into half-moon bays and mountain peaks are reduced to wave-beaten islands and stacks.

Although the land is subsiding, a mountain platform still makes up the coast's backdrop. The mountains are mantled by the 300-square-mile Harding Icefield. The icefield was not discovered until the early twentieth century when a mapping team realized that several coastal glaciers belonged to the same system. Today's icefield measures about 35 by 20 miles, whose nearly flat, snow-clad surface is interrupted only by isolated mountain peaks.

The park's wildlife is as varied as its landscape. Mountain goats, moose, bears, wolverines, marmots and others live on a thin life zone between marine waters and the icefield's frozen edges. Steller sea lions frolic on rocky islands at the entrances to Aialik and Nuka Bays, while harbor seals ride the icebergs. The fjord waters are filled with Dall porpoises, sea otters and gray, humpback, killer and minke whales. The cliffs and rocky shores abound with seabirds—horned puffins, black-legged kittiwakes, common murres and, of course, gulls.

The park provides the opportunity to observe a living laboratory of change. Here plants and wildlife exist amidst the dynamic interactions of water, ice and a glacier-carved landscape relentlessly pulled down by the movement of the earth's crust.

Above right, middle: Colorful horned puffins abound on the offshore islands. They can also be seen among the cliffs and ledges on the outer coast and at the mouths of fjords.

Right: The area surrounding Ailik Bay has something for everyone—camping, mountain climbing and boating.

Far left: The rugged and steep coastline of Northwestern Lagoon in Harris Bay.

Left: The Harris Icefield is the park's dominant feature. Covering 300 square miles, the flat, snowclad icefield is interrupted by only a few mountain peaks.

Below: The image of the vivid blue ocean waters flanked by rugged peaks will be forever etched on the memories of those who visit Kenai Fjords National Park.

Kluane, Yukon Territory

Established: 1972   Acreage: 5,440,000

Kluane National Park, in the southwestern corner of the Yukon Territory, contains Canada's highest mountains and most spectacular icefields, and some of North America's most remarkable wildlife populations. The St Elias Mountains, among the most impressive in North America, run through the park in a southeasterly direction. Since the late 1800s, the mountains have been popular with mountaineers. Mount Logan, at 19,848 feet (6050 meters), is Canada's highest peak.

The extensive icefields of the St Elias form one of the world's largest non-polar glacier systems. These massive fields of ice and snow, which are sustained by moisture-laden Pacific air that flows over the mountains, are the remnants of the last Ice Age. An unusual aspect of the Steele Glacier is that it sporadically moves at a very rapid rate. It surged downhill 1601 feet (488 meters) in one month in the late 1960s. Other interesting geological features in the park are glacier-created sand dunes and deltas built by dust storms. A large delta on Kluane Lake was created in this way.

The mountains of Kluane are home to the world's largest band of Dall sheep. Caribou are found in the northern tundra uplands, and many moose roam the sub-alpine region. Mountain goats, wolves, wolverines and grizzlies also inhabit the park. The lakes and streams of the park are filled with Arctic grayling, lake trout, northern pike and ouananiche (land-locked salmon). Golden eagles soar through the skies, and ptarmigans and bluebirds (which were once common in southern Canada) nest here, too.

The southeastern section of the park boasts luxuriant vegetation—a result of the influence of the Pacific Ocean. The river valleys are dressed in white spruce, while the higher elevations are covered with lichens, dwarf birch and low shrubs. Colorful arctic flowers grow from crevices and on rocky ledges of the mountains.

During the Klondike Gold Rush of 1898, one of the routes for travellers from the Pacific was near the southeastern boundary of Kluane. After the gold rush, prospectors travelled to other parts of the Yukon, and in 1904 the North-West Mounted Police established a control post on the south shore of Kluane Lake. In 1942, Kluane Lake was the meeting point for American and Canadian crews building the Alaska Highway.

Far right: The characteristic lonesome call of the grey wolf can be heard throughout the vast reaches of Kluane National Park.

Below: Three hikers end their journey by basking in the beauty of Kathleen Lake.

Above: Reaching the summit of Mount Logan—the park's highest peak.

Right: With apparent ease, the mountain goat trots across rocky outcrops, cliffs and ledges. This one, however, prefers to take it easy for the time being.

Kobuk Valley, Alaska

Established: 1980 Acreage: 1,750,000

Kobuk Valley National Park occupies a broad valley along the central Kobuk River in northwestern Alaska, some 25 miles (40 kilometers) north of the Arctic Circle. The park sits in a semi-enclosed bowl, ringed on the north by the Baird Mountains and lined on the south by the Waring Mountains. It is a complex mix of tundra, forest and forest tundra. No National Park Service facilities, trails or services exist in the park. People who venture to Kobuk Valley are usually interested in backpacking in the mountains and along their foothills and valleys.

Today's dry, cold climate of the Kobuk Valley still approximates that of late Pleistocene times, supporting a remnant flora once marking the vast Arctic steppe tundra bridging Alaska and Asia. Great herds of caribou still cross the Kobuk River at Onion Portage, and are hunted by Eskimos. The valley remains an important area for traditional subsistence harvest of moose, bears, caribou, fish, waterfowl and many edible and medicinal plants. The winters in Kobuk Valley are long and cold; summers are warm, but brief, and they herald the arrival of the mosquito.

The Great Kobuk Sand Dunes and the Little Kobuk Sand Dunes extend over 25 square miles (40 square kilometers) south of the Kobuk River, the former being the largest active dune field in Arctic latitudes. They can be reached by an easy hike from the river. River boat trips down the placid Kobuk River are an enjoyable way to experience the park. The Salmon River, which flows swiftly from the mountains to the Kobuk, offers the chance for canoeing and kayaking. The waters of the park are inhabited by grayling, Arctic sheer and several species of salmon.

Far right: One does not normally associate beaches with Alaska, but sand dunes are one of the hallmarks of Kobuk Valley National Park.

Facing page: When European settlers first came to North America, the grizzly bear roamed over most of the western United States and Canada. Today, its range is primarily limited to wilderness areas in Alaska, Montana, Wyoming and western Canada.

Below: Contrast this image of the dog team with the photo above. Alaska is a land of many faces, from sand dunes to frozen tundra.

Lake Clark, Alaska

Established: 1980   Acreage: 2,874,000

Located along the western shore of Cook Inlet, the isolated Lake Clark National Park and Preserve provides an unparalleled look at the diverse ecosystems of Alaska. Within the park, the mountains of the Alaska and Aleutian ranges meet, and between them stand the rugged and awesome Chigmit Mountains, formed by centuries of earthquakes and glacial action. Two active volcanoes, Iliamna and Redoubt, rising more than 10,000 feet (3050 meters) are located on the eastern side of the park.

The mountains descend rapidly to Cook Inlet, amid rivers cascading dramatically to the sea through forests of Sitka and white spruce. The coastal cliffs, holding fossil remnants of 150 million years of sea life, provide rookeries for puffins, cormorants, kittiwakes and other seabirds. Swans and other waterfowl nest on the marshes and outwash plains, while seals and whales can sometimes be seen off shore.

The western flank of the Chigmit Mountains descends through tundra-covered foothills to boreal forest. The lakes and wild rivers of the valleys abound with rainbow trout, Dolly Varden trout, lake trout, northern pike, Arctic grayling and five species of salmon. Dall sheep, caribou, moose, brown and black bear, wolves, lynx, foxes and other mammals inhabit the forests, hills and valleys. The western side of the park offers numerous recreational activities—hiking, fishing, river running and camping.

The wild, spectacular scenery of Lake Clark National Park and Preserve is accessible almost exclusively by small aircraft. Float planes can land on the many lakes throughout the region, and wheeled planes can land on open beaches, gravel bars or private airstrips in or near the park.

Winter at Lake Clark is long and harsh, with temperatures often plummeting to -40 degrees Fahrenheit. Ice break-ups in the spring can immobilize the area, but summer is the time of life as caribou calve, buds turn to leaves and salmon return to spawn.

Though the area has been inhabited since prehistoric times, it remains sparsely populated. Tanaina Indians lived in villages at Kijik and Old Village until the early 1900s. Russian explorers, traders and missionaries first discovered the land in the 1790s. In the early 1900s the salmon industry drew American, as well as foreign, settlers. In recent years, commercial fishing and recreational activities have provided economic support for the area.

Below: Still, blue lakes, tall stands of boreal spruce and snow-capped mountains—such scenic diversity makes up Lake Clark National Park.

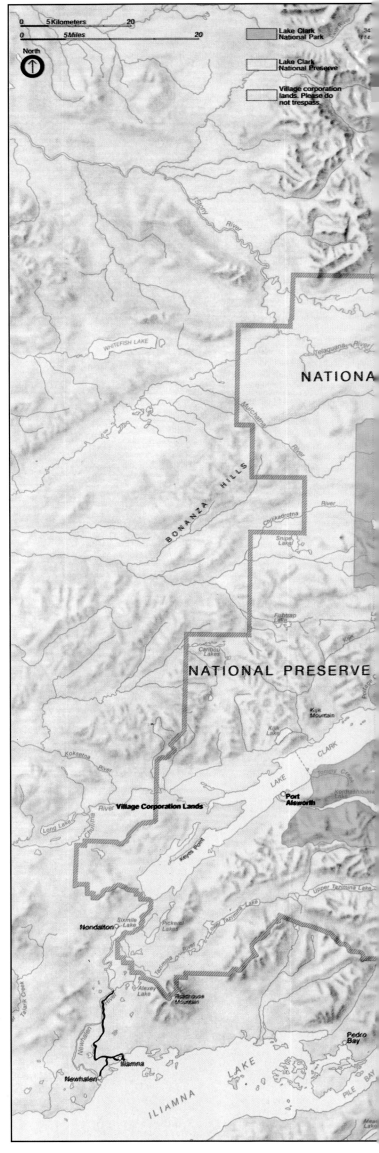

Nahanni, Northwest Territories

Established: 1972 Acreage: 1,777,600

Nahanni is a wilderness area containing the major part of the South Nahanni, one of North America's finest wild rivers. Draining an area of more than 22,370 square miles (36,00 square kilometers), the South Nahanni watershed has strikingly different landscapes. The upper reaches flow through tundra-capped mountains inhabited by mountain goats, Dall sheep and caribou. At the northern edge of the park rise the peaks of the Ragged Range, location of Hole-in-the-Wall Lake and a hot spring. In the valley below, water from Rabbitkettle Hot Springs has formed a succession of terraces more than 88 feet (27 meters) high.

The major waterfall on the South Nahanni is Virginia Falls, where the river plunges more than 298 feet (91 meters). Twice the height of Niagara Falls and the most awe-inspiring undeveloped waterfall in Canada, it shows more than three vertical acres of waterface shrouded in mist. Tumultuous rapids and whirlpools below the waterfall mark the river's journey through a constriction known as Hell's Gate. Below Hell's Gate, the Nahanni joins the Flat River, its largest tributary.

Later in its course, the South Nahanni passes near Yohin Lake. This shallow, marshy lake is the ideal habitat for large numbers of waterfowl and an unusual growth of plants. Over 40 plants not previously recorded in the surrounding area have been found in the park. Wild mint, goldenrod, yellow money-flower and aster grow in abundance near the Flat River. A lush garden of orchids grows near Virginia Falls.

The river valleys are thick with white spruce and balsam poplar, while black spruce predominate at the higher altitudes and on the northern slopes. On the higher mountains, sedges,

lichens, grasses and shrubs blanket the alpine tundra. These high mountain regions are home to Dall sheep.

More than 40 species of mammals inhabit the park. Moose and beaver live in the forested river valleys, and woodland caribou are found in the upper valleys. Black bear and deer have also been spotted in Nahanni. The park waters boast at least 13 species of fish, including Dolly Varden trout and Arctic grayling. Well over 100 species of birds—golden eagle, Canada goose and wandering tattler to name a few— grace the skies of Nahanni.

The earliest inhabitants of the Nahanni area might have been Asiatics who were lured across the Bering Strait by abundant fish and game. Two nomadic Athapaskan tribes— the Slavey and the Nahanni, meaning 'people over there far away'—lived here as late as the eighteenth century. Early in the 1800s, the Northwest Company, and later the Hudson's Bay Company, established trading posts along the Mackenzie River to support the fur trade, and the nomadic ways of the Indians ended.

Below: Awesome Virginia Falls—where the South Nahanni plunges almost 300 feet (roughly 90 meters).

Above left: A young golden eagle soars majestically in the northern skies.

Above: Dall sheep, a cousin of the larger bighorn sheep, live in the alpine tundra areas of the park.

Left: Canoeing down the Nahanni River in summer. Though placid here, the waters become quite rough.

Northern Yukon, Yukon Territory

Established: 1984   Acreage: 2,471,830

Northern Yukon National Park represents the first national park arising from the settlement of comprehensive land claims and is dedicated to wilderness preservation and the maintenance of aboriginal lifestyles. The park encompasses a wilderness on the North Slope in the northwestern corner of Yukon Territory. The North Slope rises gently from the Beaufort coastal plain into the British Mountains, which dominate most of the park.

The park contains exceptional examples of cultural and natural resources. The Engigstciak, an archaeological site on the Firth River coastal plain, is considered one of the most important archaeological resources in the western Arctic region. The site shows over 5000 years of occupation by nine different cultures, including all known Inuit cultures.

The vegetation diversity, including Arctic tundra, alpine tundra and the northern limit of the taiga, provides an excellent habitat for wildlife. Moose, Dall sheep, musk-ox and barren ground caribou roam here. The Porcupine Caribou herd is the park's most prominent wildlife feature and is one of the world's largest herds at over 150,000 animals. Three bear species of North America—black, grizzly and the endangered polar bear—are all found here. The coastal plain provides critical nesting, staging and molting areas for snow geese and whistling swans, and the park rivers also provide critical spawning grounds for Arctic char.

Far right: Northern Yukon National Park probably has the greatest diversity of wildlife of all of Canada's arctic regions. Moose are just one of the large mammals found here.

Facing page: The ferocious polar bear is well-suited to life in the freezing cold of the far north. Its thick, long coat covers even the soles of its feet, and beneath the skin lies a thick layer of fat—up to four inches thick—that insulates as well as provides energy.

Below: The ice-clogged Firth River eases its way through Northern Yukon National Park.

Wrangell-St Elias, Alaska

Established: 1980   Acreage: 8,945,000

Referred to as 'North America's mountain kingdom,' Wrangell-St Elias boggles the imagination. The number and scale of everything is enormous—peaks upon peaks, glaciers after glaciers. Three of Alaska's seven principle mountain ranges, the Wrangell, Chugach and St Elias, converge here. The park contains nine of the 16 highest peaks in the United States. Mount St Elias, its highest peak at 18,008 feet, is second only to Mount McKinley among all in the United States. To the east the park borders huge Kluane National Park in the Yukon Territory of Canada. Together they easily form the largest national park area in the world. The total acreage of Wrangell-St Elias alone makes this the largest United States national park, the size of six Yellowstones! Beyond this, it contains a representative sampling of the state's wildlife, and old mining sites indicative of man's early explorations here.

The high country is covered with snow the year round, resulting in extensive icefields and glaciers. The Bagley Icefield near the coast is the largest subpolar icefield in North America and spawns such giant glaciers as the Tana, Miles, Hubbard and Guyot. The Malaspina Glacier flows out of the St Elias Range between Ice Bay and Yakutat Bay in a mass larger than the state of Rhode Island.

Though the vegetation may seem sparse, the park has a variety of wildlife. Dall sheep and mountain goats patrol the craggy peaks; herds of caribou feed on the lichen and low, woody plants around the Wrangells; moose browse in sloughs and bogs in the coastal lowlands and in brushy areas, which also attract brown and grizzly bears. Black bear also inhabit the park. Herds of bison roam the Copper and Chitina River valleys, and sea mammals, including sea lions and harbor seals, frolic along the coast. The park waters provide spawning grounds for salmon and other fish. The Copper River drainage and the Malaspina forelands are major flyways for migratory birds, and make prime nesting areas for the majestic trumpeter swan.

Around the turn of the century Caucasians arrived in search of an all-American route to the Klondike. Their journals depict tales of deadly starvation and deprivation while trying to navigate through a seemingly impregnable mountain barrier. The more observant miners noticed the native Athabascans using tools and wearing jewelry made entirely of copper. The ensuing scramble for minerals produced one of the world's richest copper deposits at Kennecott. In the early 1900s the Kennecott Mining Company transported copper from its mines near McCarthy by railroad along the Chitina and Copper rivers to ships at Cordova. Ore was extracted from these productive mines between 1911 and 1938. Today, backpacking, mountaineering, river running, sea kayaking, fishing, and sightseeing, as well as sport and subsistence hunting, are popular activities within the park and preserve.

Above right, top: The snow never melts in the high country of the park, creating a year-round winter wonderland of icefields and glaciers.

Above right, center: The Root Glacier, not far from the town of McCarthy, population 10.

Right: In spite of its harsh environment, the park supports a wide variety of wildlife, including harbor seals.

Facing page: Wrangell-St Elias is a land of superlatives. Pictured here is but one of the park's imposing glaciers.

INDEX

Photo Credits

Overleaf: Like a jewel in the sky, the sun sparkles through the mist at La Mauricie in Quebec.